Mestra the Shapeshifter

Ancient Heroine of the Sacred Grove

Mestra the Shapeshifter

Ancient Heroine of the Sacred Grove

Dianna Rhyan

**MOON
BOOKS**

London, UK
Washington, DC, USA

CollectiveInk

First published by Moon Books, 2024
Moon Books is an imprint of Collective Ink Ltd.,
Unit 11, Shepperton House, 89 Shepperton Road, London, N1 3DF
office@collectiveinkbooks.com
www.collectiveinkbooks.com
www.moon-books.net

For distributor details and how to order please visit the 'Ordering' section on our website.

Text copyright: Dianna Rhyan 2023

ISBN: 978 1 80341 529 1
978 1 80341 673 1 (ebook)
Library of Congress Control Number: 2023945775

A CIP catalogue record for this book is available from the British Library.

Design: Lapiz Digital Services

UK: Printed and bound by CPI Group (UK) Ltd, Croydon, CR0 4YY
Printed in North America by CPI GPS partners

We operate a distinctive and ethical publishing philosophy in all areas of our business, from our global network of authors to production and worldwide distribution.

Contents

To Nicholas
palikari

For Mark
philotimos

Eros invincible, you rest unconquered,
sleeping gentle nights on a maiden's soft cheek.
Then up you soar, above vast wilderness and over stormy sea.
(Sophocles, Antigone)

Preface

When we look back to the women of archaic myth, we find so many stories in fragments. This book gathers the pieces of ancient papyrus where the mysterious shapeshifter Mestra appears, places these clues in your hands, and invites you to follow her sacred journey, letting your imagination run wild with her, like wind in the trees or waves in the sounding sea.

Mestra's path of metamorphosis is always open to discovery. Her creativity, her cunning, and her circle of spiritual sisters may mirror your own. What transformative potential is she gesturing toward for you?

DR

Chapter 1

Mysteries of Mestra

Mestra did not start life as a shapeshifter, or a heroine.

She walked the earth and swam the sea of distant long ago as a mortal woman, who may have seemed like a simple girl at first yet bore a mysterious fate. Famed for her cleverness and beauty, beloved of Demeter and Poseidon, she was a magical maiden, a sacred oak votary – and an untamed animal when she had to be. She lived by innocence, then by cunning, and became a shapeshifter by necessity. Her metamorphic adventures celebrate self-transformation, a vibrant potential in all of us.

> She could become anything, anything at all,
> changing herself into every shape and every form.
> Raging lioness or bristling boar,
> sinuous fish, bull with massive horns,
> fearlessly winging bird, skimming the tips of the waves.
> Mestra had this power.
> (Catalogue; Alcman; Ovid's Metamorphoses)[1]

As her path opens, she leads the way to forbidden groves, feral animals, wily tricksters, and capricious deities who reveal compelling truths. The maiden who becomes a trickster, divine consort, mare, heifer, and bird is no mere figment of myth. Mestra represents the outermost and innermost limits of human experience, a fertile capacity for radical change, that is always emergent in our psyche, even if it is sometimes dormant or hidden away. Beside her, watered by springs with the power to awaken, nurtured at knees of sacred trees, prophetic priestesses and nymphs await.

Mountain-born, pure of voice, fleet of foot,
they dance and sing in exquisite worship, circling dark
  waters,
springs rising deep beneath shadowing boughs,
and divine Echo joins their song, sighing through rocky
  peaks.
(Homeric Hymn to Pan)

Like divine Echo, whose melodious voice lingers among remote peaks and secluded caverns, Mestra's elusive story has all but vanished. While some heroines survive in a multitude of ancient sources, the fascination of Mestra lies more in her layered veils of obscurity that hide her from view. I never heard of her until I started studying the fragmentary and lost epics of archaic Greece. Since the scraps of evidence for her life are few, anyone who wants to follow her must shift into sleuth form to sift the ancient signs.

Where to start? In a sacred grove. From childhood, she was a devotee of the goddess Demeter.

There once was a sacred grove of Demeter,
and in the very center stood a statuesque oak,
A goddess grown centuries green.
The reach of her boughs made a shadowy precinct,
sheltering manifold life within her being.
All around her limbs were woven votive offerings:
woolen ribbons, wreaths of flowers,
homemade garlands from feminine hands,
signs of her power to grant prayers.

Often in her shade dryads led their festive dances –
nymphs whose lives were the lives of their trees.
Linking slender wrists, holding hands,
the dancing nymphs would circle her mighty trunk.

Ancestral to all the trees surrounding,
her shade gently wafted down, just as
the dryads' shadows over the soft green grass
moved tenderly on bare feet.
(*Metamorphoses*)

In Mestra's alignment with Demeter, founding goddess of the ancient world's mightiest mystery cult, it is rightly said for the goddess, her sacred oak, the grove, the nymphs, and Mestra:

they shelter manifold life within their being.

Outside the grove, by birth rather than by choice, Mestra was a princess of Thessaly, daughter of Erysichthon, a prince infamous for his violence against the sacred grove, and his tragic downfall afterward. Cursed by Demeter for his hubris, for purposely felling the goddess's beloved tree, he was doomed to ravenous hunger. His relentless appetite brought shame to his family and laid waste to all the goods of his house. In the end, Erysichthon consumed himself to meet his grisly end. Before that extremity, the hard-hearted father stooped to using his daughter Mestra to purchase food, marrying her off repeatedly to spend the proceeds, bride-prices given for her hand.

Yet all was not lost for Mestra. She devised secret stratagems to escape these transactions and avoided her father's doom. On the brink of her wedding, already veiled for the ceremony, she made a bold discovery. She discovered she could shapeshift, flee, and then find herself again.

A stately eagle among a flock of birds,
a tiny ant hiding in a seething nest,
an entire swarm of shimmering bees in flight,
a dread, coldblooded viper.
(*Catalogue*)

5

Within herself, she had found a form of protection, evasive action against unwanted weddings. Spiritually, she had found much more. She could unite opposite forces and embody primal elements of nature:

> Now she was rippling water engulfing a dam,
> now she was water's deadly opponent, insatiable flame.
> *(Catalogue; Metamorphoses)*

The moment she unearthed her ability to self-transform, she left behind mortal rules, and opened infinite routes of escape. They might imprison a maiden, but no bonds could hold her as a venomous serpent, surging wave, or scorching flame. Her manifold forms, her veiled and secretive journey, ultimately led to her unveiling in sacred union with the divine.

> Honey-voiced Muses of Olympus,
> sing the sweet song of distant long ago,
> of mortal women remembered for their brilliance:
> daughters of kings who loosened their garments,
> and mated with gods.
> *(Hesiod, Theogony)*

Renowned for her cunning, mingling with a god, Mestra evaded expectations, casting aside the form of a girl. The cultural frameworks she dodged determined female footsteps with carefully choreographed control. But not her footsteps; not anymore.

> Suddenly she took on whatever shape she imagined:
> melodious wren building a hidden nest,
> filly skittish of any halter,
> wary and willowy doe,
> snarling panther, lone howl of midnight wolf.

Mestra's shapeshifting skill places her among wondrous beings of world mythology who are mystical, legendary, and folkloric. Yet in all that survives of classical myth from Greece and Rome, she is the only ancient heroine who transforms herself through her own power. Ancient gods and goddesses changed their forms at will. But for lesser beings, metamorphosis came from without rather than from within, when they found themselves changed by a deity. Many endured metamorphoses unwillingly, and then lived on fixed in their new shape forever.

> Io once maid now a wandering heifer,
> Arachne spinning as a spider,
> Calisto prowls through the stars as a bear.
> Arethusa surges as a gushing spring,
> Niobe's tears pour down a rock face.
> Blooming Narcissus leans beside the mirrored pool,
> Syrinx lifts her reed voice on the shore.
> Medusa and Scylla lurk in their caves,
> Orion strides the constellations,
> hunter among the stars.

Mestra is not one of those. By freely transforming herself into animals, humans, and elements, she entered a province of divine power. Before she ever loved a sea god, Mestra became like a slippery sea deity herself:

> Now she was a whirlpool or swirling undertow,
> now a smooth skinned eel or dolphin sleek.
> Such was silver-footed Thetis,
> mist shrouded sea goddess, naiad of the deep.
> Such was Proteus, ancient sage of the sea,
> who plunged through the waters that embrace the world.
> (Metamorphoses)

In time, Mestra's approach to immortal potency grew intimate. Her fame spread. Her crafty metamorphic guises and beauty attracted her divine lover, the ever shifting and boundlessly passionate sea god Poseidon. Having rejected a multitude of suitors, she chose to couple with the ultimate masculine principle of shapeshifting, the Sea who seethes with fertile forms, attaining unknowable hidden depths.

Some said Poseidon abducted her. Or did she speed across the dark waters of Oceanus by his side as a long-winged seabird?

From her beginning in Demeter's sacred grove, to our final glimpse of her as she disappears from our sight forever over the sea, Mestra knows joys and sorrows. She embodies many contrasts, and however we might invoke her, by her very nature she will be fleetingly present, then subtly shift her form and slip away.

Honey-voiced Muses and archaic poets acclaimed her greatest feature: her supple, polymorphic mind. Hailed as exceedingly perceptive, endowed with keen intuition, and experienced in many likenesses, she considered the shapeshifting god Poseidon when he desired her, matched him in a battle of wits, and made him prove his mettle. Poets hailed her as a heroine, a word of many meanings. In Mestra's case, they meant a woman who performed memorable deeds and transcended mortality by virtue of more-than-mortal gifts, including wily resourcefulness, radiance, and grace.[2]

An archaic heroine might, for example, possess a face that launched a thousand ships (Helen), wait faithfully for a husband while outwitting one hundred and eight suitors (Penelope), be deserted as a princess yet deified as a goddess (Ariadne), come to life as a lovely snare to avenge a Titan's theft of fire (Pandora), or narrowly escape being slaughtered on the altar of her own wedding (Iphigeneia). Or she might outwit her sacrilegious father, elude a multitude of suitors, shapeshift at will, mate with a god, and bear a semidivine son (Mestra). After death, a woman who transformed into a heroine moved somewhere between mortals and the divine. She was empowered to help or harm mortals, honored as an illustrious ancestor, and potentially worshipped in a cult. It was wise to revere her resting place, dedicate offerings at sites where she suffered or loved, and remember her in myth and prayer. Veneration warded off her anger, and evoked the gracious favors her eternal spirit might bestow.

For a moment, it seemed the ruined sanctuary rose, stately stones molded in mossy green shadows, pale robes of dryads, boughs adorned with shimmering textiles, the flash of crimson ribbons, votive garlands fluttering in the breeze. Place on her head the tower headdress, fortification of the city — yet wreathe her also with softest spring blossoms. She is proceeding. What shall we offer her? Always, first of the fruits, first of the earliest blooming flowers, shy beauties. Dusty avenues are sprinkled with petals, cooled by watercarriers, filled with a throng of maidens and youths, whose songs float up to the sky. Amid her joyous worshipers, leaving her sanctuary and returning, there moves the goddess's chariot, for the cyclical renewal that is hers, and the seasonal renewal of all the land.[3]

Mestra shares mythic features with Helen, Penelope, Ariadne, Pandora, and Iphigeneia, but differs in one essential element. On her way to becoming a heroine, Mestra discovers her metamorphic potential, and first becomes a different kind of mysterious entity. Not a monster, goddess, sorceress, witch, or nymph; something closer to a *daimon*.

A *daimon* was many things to the ancient Greek psyche: a spirit, deep-seated emotion, impulse, force of nature, spirit, heroine/hero, supernatural agent of fate, or divinity who impacted humans on a visceral level.[4] Sometimes a *daimon* was a deity or nymph who did have a name, but it was better to leave them unnamed for the moment. Or perhaps their identity was not entirely clear. Able to traverse great distances with awe-inspiring velocity and sway the balance of a human life, *daimones* could incite mortals to delusion, desire, panic, hunger, valor, inspiration, or sudden bouts of conscience; or they could simply enjoy their freedom in the cosmos, residing somewhere between deities and humankind. Naturally, they could shapeshift.

In this way shapeshifting Athena first appeared to the son of Odysseus in Homer's *Odyssey*:

> So spoke the grey-eyed goddess in the shape of a mortal man.
> But suddenly she changed her form again and departed,
> leaping up into flight like a bird silhouetted against the sky.
> She placed in his heart a new and vigorous spirit,
> and he rose with a new courage,
> boldness he had not sensed before her arrival.
> Struck with wonder by her metamorphosis,
> he pondered this astonishment in his heart,
> thinking he had truly encountered a divine being.

As Socrates described passionate Eros, he was a *daimon* who possessed hearts with the flutter of passionate love. As a winged shapeshifter Eros is never still:

> Ever changeable, ever becoming, always reviving, and always fading away.
> (*Plato, Symposium*)

Likewise Sleep and Death materialized on the battlefield in the *Iliad*:

> Sleep and Death, twin brothers, winged,
> came from afar, descending.

They carried Zeus' son,
over dark lands and misty seas,
the hero bravely fallen in battle,
to his honored memorial.

Daimones appeared and disappeared more swiftly than human thought, more softly than human perception:

Their tender feet do not go near the ground.
Traversing the air above mortals' heads,
they arrive and depart on noiseless wings.
(*Iliad*)

Not at the beginning of her life, but later, Mestra became capable of such flight. How did she gain her powers?

It was a *daimon* who set Mestra's journey in motion, in the form of a sentient tree.

Mestra's story begins with this tree, the gigantic oak we met earlier in the center of the sacred grove. She was the "goddess grown centuries green," a holy elder in tree form who held sway over human destinies.

As *daimon* of the region,
watching protectively over the land,
the oak spirit was favorable to the ruling dynasty.

But when the grove was shamefully disrespected,
the *daimon* grew wrathful,
and woeful misfortune prevailed.
(*Callimachus, Hymn to Demeter*)

The phrase "*daimon* of the region" reminds us that all of creation is alive and ensouled with nymphs. Mystical caves, spacious dancing grounds, gushing streams, fertile meadows, and echoing valleys are imbued with divine indwelling spirits. So are seashores, forests, bears, panthers, deer, and wolves.

So sang the mythic poet Orpheus:

> He sang how in the beginning,
> all things fitted together in one form:
> how mountains rose into the light,
> how rivers that roar and creatures that walk
> were born on the earth with their indwelling nymphs.
> (Apollonius of Rhodes, *Voyage of Argo*)

When the holy oak fell to Erysichthon's devouring axe, it was by becoming a *daimon* herself that Mestra narrowly escaped falling victim to his madness. The daughter who was unable openly to resist royal and paternal power turned to stealth, summoned her creativity, and aligned with the potency of tree and water to survive. Her love of forest and sea protected her.

As we watch her elude betrothals, her rites of passage lead from joyful rituals in a garlanded grove to renewal in the expansive sovereignty of the mystical sea. Although she may have faltered, she never forgot the greenwood, where she was never alone.

Look for her around the circle of nature spirits, harmonious and flowering nymphs:

> Their joy is the flourishing of noble trees.
> As they dance with the winds, springtime flourishes,
> in their graceful bodies and the gentle season.
> Daughters, mothers, and nymphs together,
> when warm breezes blow and cold winter disappears,
> drape themselves in glistening veils, and step lightly on the
> earth.

Heroines fair of brow gaze up at clear heavens that pasture
the stars.
Like beautifully maned horses, they shake loose luxurious
tresses,
and divine fragrance wafts around their robes.
Companions wreathed in violets,
frolicking in divine joy, they are spirits set free, and
immortals walk among them.
(*Catalogue*)

There she is in the sacred grove, holding hands, dancing in the
season of glorious youth. Yet she steps outside the circle too.
In ancient sources, Mestra often stands just outside the frame
of perception, relegated to a supporting role, eclipsed by her
father's notoriety, or anonymous, omitted from her own story,
invisible.

Is the periphery where she chooses to be? Perhaps. If we
return to her origin, her Greek name speaks. It meant Clever or
Cunning, suggesting a naming by fate, a name she is destined
to live out to the fullest, flowing between forms, in and out of
darkness, often in disguise.

Around the open-air altar, entwined with her in multiple
consciousness, there range primordial goddesses, dancing
dryads, and eloquent trees: *daimones* who all play a role in
Mestra's mysteries. We will meet Mestra's allies, including
Demeter, Persephone, Hera, Thetis, Artemis, the Graces, the
Doves, Dione Naia, Nemesis, Athena, Arachne, Ino-Leukothea,
Io, Pandora, Iphigeneia, Ariadne, Penelope, Aphrodite, Tethys,
and primordial Earth. All these sisters who illuminate her
journey.

If we explore mythic metamorphosis, we are also plumbing
the gifts of fairytale, omen, spirit journey, intuition, magic,
shamanism, and dream. If we breathe life into Mestra's
fragments, we invite her wholeness into our consciousness. And

once we grow curious about her shadows, we meet on shadowy paths aspects of ourselves that have fallen silent.

Silent as forsaken groves and abandoned holy trees? Why have their words fled away?

Well, Mestra's father Erysichthon was a prince of princely appetites.

> A man who scorned the gods,
> and bought no incense,
> no offering, to any altar.

When he comes face to face with the holy oak in the sanctuary, he sees her limbs festooned with votive offerings, witnesses her eminence in the sacred precinct, and beholds her numinous power. When the bite of the axe begins, he hears the admonition of Demeter's high priestess. He even hears the oak utter human speech and wail in lamentation, and hears the dryad curse him for his desecration. Still,

> he couldn't have cared less.
> (*Metamorphoses*)

Tone-deaf to reverence, Erysichthon encounters the majestic oak and feels...nothing. His merciless scorn for the spiritual traditions that nurtured him leads him to destroy the sacred landscape of his birth. In the end, his utter ruin, devised by tree, priestess, dryad, goddess, and *daimon*, makes for memorable poetry.

His daughter is memorable in a different way; that proverbial apple fell far from the tree. With the sacred grove in her heart, Mestra opposes Erysichthon's values, and this defiant, innovative, and determined female outmaneuvers authoritarian rule, to find not tragedy but harmony in the end.

Among the countless women whose names have vanished in the mists of antiquity, we may be thankful that Mestra's name survived. Discovered on tattered scraps of papyrus and plucked out of oblivion for remembrance, much of her story was excavated in scattered fragments that were found in an ancient garbage heap. Fortunately, she was intriguing from the very beginning, thousands of years ago, in all her manifold forms. It seems especially fitting for a shapeshifter that her story circulated in ever-changing versions.

How did she make her way from the ancient world to us today? Mestra lived in Thessaly, Athens, or on the island of Cos. She descended (in a line replete with magical beings and monsters) from Deucalion and Pyrrha, who were in Greek myth the sole survivors of the Flood. Her earliest myth scarcely survived, in a ragged papyrus list of long-ago mothers of heroes: a gap-riddled resource of female ancestry disconcertingly known as the Hesiodic *Catalogue of Women*.[5] She surfaces again in Callimachus' *Hymn to Demeter* (though she is offstage and unnamed). To make her way from Greece to Rome, she enters Ovid's epic *Metamorphoses*, in the yarn of a shapeshifting river god admirer. As late as the nineteenth century CE, a Greek folktale still featured a dryad who was murdered in her tree and avenged upon a guilty prince; the dryad's name was "Little Demeter," an oblique survival of Mestra's story. Other ancient clues and passing mentions remain. Some name her a sorceress for her magical gift of transformation; some manage to pack broad accusations into scanty words, claiming Mestra was a "vixen," hinting she was a brazen prostitute.

A sorceress who could metamorphose into the shape of any
    animal,
her father used her to save himself from starvation.

Or then again:

A bright-tailed vixen (i.e., prostitute) who could take on any
form,
her earnings went to feed her father every day.[6]

Over time, viewed as a female with suspect talents and motives,
she became a forgotten curiosity. Today, if we look though
mythological indexes, though her father appears, Mestra
mostly isn't there. But originally, in the frayed and threadbare
manuscripts, Mestra was the heroine of her own story.

In search of her, I interweave all versions of her myth and
delve wherever possible for clues. Each chapter will explore a
different aspect of Mestra, creatively woven around a particular
glimpse of her that shines through in her scant fragments.
The resulting whole is one way to honor her story. There are
other ways to reconstruct the tattered evidence, other ways to
reassemble her portrait; I convey what I found most inspiring.

Mestra's sojourns will inspire travels of our own, transporting
us to other places and times – as she was divinely transported.
We will visit oracles, glades, sacred enclosures, and seashores,
attuning our hearts to ancient voices.

Travelers, gather around the altar,
make a ring around the sacred dancing ground to hear.
Maidens of fair voice, dedicated to farseeing Apollo,
sing wondrous hymns to the gods,
enchanting the hearts of listening crowds.
Then they sing a song of remembrance,
of men and women who lived long ago.
(Homeric Hymn to Apollo)

Mestra was one of their songs.

In ancient days, travelers embarked on distant journeys
to hear choruses of maidens sing in sacred groves. They
undertook quests to gardens or tombs of heroines. Thirsting

16

for communion and refreshment of the soul, seekers left their loveliest possessions as offerings, to honor the indwelling spirits of the place:

> Hail, welling spring, pure fountain!
> Your nymphs offer honeyed water from delicate hands.
> I, a traveler, immersed in your clear, cold stream
> this precious cup, my very best, to refresh my thirst.
> Now, among the carved images of nymphs
> dedicated and drenched by your streams,
> I leave it for you as an offering.
> (Greek Anthology)[7]

So we travelers make our beginning.

Mestra reminds us that what is fallen will gather strength, and what is overlooked and imprisoned will find the way to rise again. She points a way to resistance against conformity and escape from authoritarian rule. On her archetypal sojourn, the conscious grove and sea respond to her, and respond to us if we will follow. She is the embodiment of fluid psychology, and her triumph of supple imagination calls us to contemplate the changes of inherently unpredictable life.

When she appears, imagination heals and enchantment reigns. Across millennia she captivates with forgotten longings, ancient wisdom, goddess traditions, esoteric knowledge, tree worship, multiple consciousness, nature spirituality, trickster and shapeshifter lore, and the mysteries of regeneration after failure and loss. A complex list for a complex being.

Rediscovering her, we uncover our own transformative and transforming selves.

> She had urgent stories to tell so she sang like a nightingale,
> docile manners to kick away so she turned into a mule,

places she wanted to see so she became the wandering wind,
questing curiosity so she became a root,
a diving fish to feel the water on her skin,
delicate doe darting lightly away from her captors.

Contemplating her ever-changing image can be a creative act of devotion and self-discovery if we so choose.[8]

What is the experience of discovering another self, hidden within the one you thought you already knew? Even when cloaked or caged, how powerful are our submerged instincts and subconscious minds? Encounter Mestra, and suddenly we are dancing on the undulating lines between. She invites us to slip the collar and spring open the cage, to swim with swelling tides and dance in sacred groves. To distrust tyrants who bear bridles in their hands, listen to the trees we encounter, and dream of shores unseen. To draw on a canny modern title, Mestra invites us to move between "women who run with the wolves" and a woman who becomes one.[9]

Chapter 2

Oak and Dove

There once was a vast, fair grove,
a grove Demeter loved with passion.
Spreading far and wide, thickly forested,
standing so abundant with trees that
no arrow could pass through in flight.
Inside grew lofty pines, mighty elms, and stately oaks,
fertile wild pears, and blushing sweet apples.
There flowed rivulets, streams shining bright as electrum.
(Callimachus, Hymn to Demeter)

Divinities gather here, fair as the trees. Mestra moves among them. Under flickering leaves, immortals offer the refreshment of pure water and just-ripe apples, drawing us closer, toward the elemental. Demeter passionately loves this sheltered glade. Yet she is a goddess experienced in grief. And look. Just as we approach the cooling shade that shelters wondrous charms, the image of a flying arrow appears. No one should shoot an arrow into a holy forest, where the penalty of hunting could be death. Why begin with an image so exquisite, yet so hauntingly full of foreboding?

This poignant landscape expresses the long, deep foreknowing of a forest faced with shortsighted human invasion.

When her royal father undertook to trespass in Demeter's sanctuary, Mestra was not there. Erysichthon had failed to mention his plans. Why speak of such things with women? He found a time when worshippers were absent, especially avoiding his daughter, for he knew this consecrated forest was where she most belonged. Long before her father turned his mind to this place, Mestra intimately knew the grove, and the grove knew her.

Here dwelt priestesses and wise women:

> In life I was a priestess of Demeter,
> in time an old woman, and now I am dust.
> I guided many young priestesses,
> through passage to new womanhood.
> Traveler, farewell.
> (Palatine Anthology)

From girlhood, Mestra worshiped in this enclosure, entering with her mother at propitious times to leave votive statuettes, clothing, textiles, or dolls as offerings to tree-clad goddesses. She played a prominent role in ritual here, a noble maiden serving her local cult. As votary to the virgin grove, ever more confident as seasons slipped by, she followed and then ventured to lead the maiden chorus of song and dance.

> After bathing and smoothing their skin with shining olive oil,
> they shared a meal along the grassy riverbank.
> Then they threw off their veils to play, and it was she who led out the dancing.
> She was like Artemis, who haunts remote mountain peaks,
> sighting wild boars and racing with the deer running free.
> Along with her moved the nymphs untamed,
> who wander the trackless forest sanctuary,
> and the hearts of their mothers were gladdened.
> A blossom among blossoms,
> she was radiant among her companions, a maiden unwed.
> (Odyssey)

A group of worshippers who threw off inhibitions to share in sacred rites, delighting their deity, could be called a *thiasos* or sacred throng. United by initiation, they gathered to dance, feast, drink, sing, sacrifice, pray, or lament, taking strength in torchlight or daylight processions. Together, celebrants who gathered for mystery rites, filled to overflowing with divine enthusiasm, accessed realities unavailable to the uninitiated. Mestra's *thiasos* was devoted to the festivals of Demeter.

Daylong vigil in the sacred grove.
The worshippers are parched with fasting.
Suddenly, the song begins.

Women raise their cry of welcome:
"Praise Demeter, rich in sprouting grain!"
Evening has begun to emerge from clouds on the horizon.

Sacred emblems come around the circle,
hand to hand; only the initiated may touch.

When the Evening Star rises, we will lift the goddess,
bathe and dress her image, break bread, and soothe our
thirst.

We will scatter the seeds who are her children,
link hands in circle dances,
worshippers rejoicing in the nourisher of many,
singing praise to her manifold forms.
(*Hymn to Demeter*)

Thiasos bonds formed inside the grove had power outside its boundaries, especially for women, whose lives were meant to be subdued. Secretly or openly, ritual connections invigorated daily life near hearths, looms, ovens, wells, bridal chambers, and childbirth beds. Here in the grove, girls grew closer as they moved through the stages of life together, and learned from priestesses, dryads, and trees.

The oak grove embraces Mestra's *thiasos* because the trees form a *thiasos* too.

A drift of transparent milkweed alights on the oak's mounded, muscled bark. The priestess of Demeter nods. This is what gentleness is.

Kneel and scoop it up, cradling the tendrils, and you can't feel the fluff in your palm; the seed is too soft. Fingers curl lightly around the gossamer to save it from crumpling; to save it from those who have given the goddess affront. An intruder has somehow come here, slashed milky vessels with a stick, then trampled them on the ground. Yet in this full moon's evening rise, in a glistening path on water, a luminous fragment floats free, downy hair streaming, muddy to her seed-waist in the moonlight. Here is the gossamer touch of fingertips lightly meeting, to move around the tree.

In the beginning, inside tree sanctuaries there stood no monumental temples of stone, no declarative tablets carved in bronze, no sacrifices of a hundred bellowing oxen. Footsteps were soft and chosen with care.

As a chorus of nymphs sense each other's steps in a dance, trees live out the plurality of fertile thiasos. Look at any forest if it is wild enough and see how all things move together in the spiral dance of life and death. This hawthorn sending out shoots to the south is embraced by a beech stretching north. Mutual care flows, with reciprocal seasons for leaf, root, twig, stump. Trees at the edge of the forest are strong in a different way from those within; they have grown together, aware of one another's needs. The row of old white pines reflected in the pond link hands underground, brushing in breezes above, swaying in wave patterns dear to themselves, alive in each other's kenning.

In the greenwood, sacred bands would gather for ceremonies to ring the forest with ephemeral songs. Their charmed listeners were youthful saplings clustered at the feet of their mother tree. All was imbued with the enchantment we call grace.

Personified and tripled in cult and myth, the ambience we call grace became the Graces. We glimpse these three goddesses beside Mestra in her most ancient surviving poetic portrait:

> Mestra of lustrous tresses cascading,
> she who shone with radiance like the Graces.
> *(Catalogue)*

Only a few words on a bit of papyrus, the merest shining fragment. Yet it is enough to show a fleeting glimpse of Mestra. Shining robes, fragrant garlands, tuneful song, and twining steps were the Graces' province, and these were their beautiful gifts to Mestra. Naturally, the Graces attended the gracious goddess Aphrodite.

> The Graces and the Seasons draped laughter-loving Aphrodite
> in raiment they sprinkled with the hue of every springtime blossom:
> golden crocus, sky-blue hyacinth, purple violet, lovely blushing rose,
> pure white narcissus, and lily, sweet as nectar, with petals of ambrosia.
> Wafting perfumes from their shimmering veils,
> they wove sweetly fragranced flowers into wreaths,
> placed them on each other's heads,
> then raised harmonious songs,
> deep in the forested slopes of Mount Ida rich in springs.
> *(Cypria)*

Mestra's alignment with the Graces, her blossoming youth, lustrous hair, and radiant expression, remind us that she will not be a girl forever and will one day come to know the goddess of love. But not yet. For now, the Graces adorn others. When budding Mestra shines like them, we see her inner nature too, and know that their essences – kindness, beauty, heartfelt gratitude, and sensual delight – are blossoming in Mestra, inside the sacred grove.

While Aphrodite reposed on Mount Ida, Demeter dwelt in her sacred grove of Thessaly near Mestra's home, where the *thiasos* adorned not the goddess of love, but the goddess of fruition.

Demeter's oak, wreathed and encircled by worshippers, fluttered with hand woven sashes and hand tied ribbons, tenderly looped textiles, veils in secret vales. These fabric offerings enfolded feminine prayers and dreams. Beside her mother at the loom, in the company of other women, Mestra helped create the holy tree's adornment, votive garlands from delicate hands.

When we pause here on the soft grass to look up afresh at the garlanded oak, are we beholding the tree, the tree goddess, or the tree's soul, her dryad? It is impossible to say. Leafy boughs and swaying spirits move gently together in the breeze and exist on a continuum with each other, as their filtered, dancing interplay steals softly into our senses.

When the dryad spoke in Mestra's story,
she spoke as the responsive soul of her tree,
the life force of the heartwood.

A dryad or tree nymph, the embodiment of her tree's life energy, uniquely joined with the tree she ensouled. Not concealed beneath the bark, but integrally woven into the fabric of the tree's life, her nymphic spirit mingles with the tree's materiality.

When lofty firs and stately oaks spring up from holy ground,
their nymphs are born in that very same hour,
and together they flourish on the breast of abundant Earth,
lifting their graceful arms to the heavens.
Mortals must never approach them with iron.
(*Homeric Hymn to Aphrodite*)

The dryad shares her tree's psyche; she invigorates its aura; and in times of crisis or festival, makes epiphany within the tree.

Dryad-tree-dryad. The first shapeshifting Mestra ever saw.

From the dawn of religion, around the Mediterranean Sea and far beyond, sanctuaries embraced a living tree as the focus of worship. Many goddesses dwelt in tree form, including Demeter, Artemis, Hera, Aphrodite, Minoan tree divinities, and the Cypriot goddess with raised arms. A trunk of bare wood, curvaceous and twisted, was called a *xoanon* if it was placed upright inside a tree shrine for veneration, sacrosanct.

A raw plank organic, never touched with chisel.[10]

Left uncarved and primal, or sometimes ritually and minimally shaped by human hand, the *xoanon*, the trunk of a tree goddess, is the goddess living beyond her ages in the forest, a focus for awe and devotion. When she received sacrifices, was carried in procession, and worshiped, the *xoanon* was strong, vibrant, and flourishing.

Like the oak in Mestra's story, each divine living tree and wooden *xoanon* held cultic titles, addressed as Divine Mistress, She Who Is Holy, or Very Holy One when awestruck worshippers spoke to her.

As we already know, she herself can speak.

Far away in the mists of time, there dwelt her elder sisters: prophetic trees who shared a primeval sacred grove, extraordinary oaks with the power of human speech. These enigmatic beings addressed mortals who journeyed far to seek their counsel. Deeply rooted in archaic Greek myth, they also lived in history as the first and only oracle existing in Greece for many years. Ancient mythographers remembered their dryads as compassionate nurses for cloud-gathering Zeus when he was in his vulnerable infancy, who shielded him and henceforth revealed his will to humankind. These sacred oaks grew in the mystical sanctuary of Dodona.

Odysseus was rumored to seek out this oracle on his far-flung wanderings, when he consulted an oak that spoke with countless leafy tongues:

> The hero has journeyed to Dodona, to hear the prophecy of
> Zeus,
> the voice of the holy oak whose tongues are a thousand
> leaves.
> He seeks to learn by what devices he could manage to return
> home,
> having been away, thought dead, for too many dangerous
> years.
> (Odyssey)

This precinct was known even at Troy to seekers of wisdom. In Homer's *Iliad* the hero Achilles prayed to Zeus of the oak grove through the mediation of unusual priests:

> Lofty Zeus, lord of Dodona, living in faraway land,
> you keep watch over the sacred precinct where your priests
> reside,
> living among the oaks and sleeping on the ground with feet
> unwashed.
> Hear me.

The oak priests were barefoot mountain dwellers who slept unsheltered amongst the trees, dreaming in conscious contact with the ground. Their practices suggest spiritual union with the oaks' chthonic power rooted deep inside the earth. They lived as rustics, holy men without pretense. And why not? Surely oaks preferred glades to buildings, and unpretentious votaries to grand officials. Likewise, some said the priestesses of the sanctuary "lived inside the hollow of an oak," or even "in a stump," suggesting wizened trees as simple shrines or habitations. An ancient truth is afoot here: unassuming wayfarers who shied away from crowded precincts were welcome in tranquil groves for hushed communion with the divine. As one Roman naturalist observed,

> In primordial times trees were understood as sacred precincts, and as temples of forest divinities. Even today, country folk, preserving simpler, purer, and older rituals, will consecrate their most majestic tree to a goddess or god. And though we may be accustomed now to see sacred statues gleaming with gold and ivory, we are still struck with adoration and awe by a glade of trees, a sacred grove veiled in utter silence. Each kind of tree is beloved forever to its own divinity: the beech to Jupiter, laurel to Apollo, olive to Minerva, myrtle to Venus, and poplar to Heracles. We have faith that all the divine forest guardians, Fauns, and all the many goddess Nymphs, are chosen by heaven to keep watch over such groves.
>
> *(Pliny the Elder, Natural History)*

Though some tree sanctuaries acquired formal shrines over time, or built a courtyard for a sacred tree, the true spirit of the place was never encased by foundations or roofed by any structure. As for temple columns, only a single pillar or *xoanon* was needed, to reflect the tree-as-goddess standing there, observing your approach.

> In the open-air shrine where Mestra walked,
> leaf canopies arched into vaulted roofs,
> yielding moss cradled bare feet.
> No need for floor or ceiling.
> Or columns either,
> for there stood Demeter's speaking oak,
> branching question marks in the wind,
> rooting answers below.

The speaking oaks of Dodona were famed for wise counsel, even when the case was desperate and the journey remote. Archaeologists have unearthed and deciphered travelers' questions and the oracle's replies, in the form of inscriptions incised on strips of lead. Seekers unburdened themselves to the oracle:

> Will my crops be fruitful?
> To what god should I pray to be free of slavery?
> To what god should she pray to bear children?
> Will my family be safe?

The oaks answered, offering resolution or hope.[11] Ancient myth remembers such meetings. When the exiled heroine Io roamed the world, the venerable trees helped her make sense of her experience.

> Maiden, you have wandered and endured as far as steep
>   Dodona,
> where grows the oracular grove of Zeus.
> There the oaks endowed with human speech,
> a portent beyond hope,

in clear and certain speech, no riddling words,
hailed you as a destined consort of Zeus.
(Aeschylus, Prometheus Bound)

Even Herakles, paragon of might, submitted to their prophetic guidance:

The final completion to the labors of Herakles,
crafted by the gods, he heard for himself at Dodona:
the ancient oak of many tongues and many voices
foretold his fate, speaking through the oak priestesses,
in the form of twin doves of the wood.
(Sophocles, Women of Trachis)

What did Odysseus, Io, Herakles, and other suppliants hear? An oak *daimon* sighing in archaic boughs, fluttering birds concealed in rustling leaves, or murmured syllables from mystic priestesses? Essences mingle to express spirits mingling on the sacred site. The doves especially draw attention here, for they represent the epiphany of the primeval Earth goddess in bird form. She loved to swoop free in flight, and relished bird epiphanies. She was a winged traveler to the limits of the ocean, mother of monsters, bringer of youthful blossoming, bearer of the day of doom, and mistress of fecund animals. Her bird and tree forms invite us to reflect on the doves of Dodona, as they nestled in deep-leaved, deep-bosomed holy oaks.

From distant Dodona sojourners come back bearing oracles:
omens of wise bird-sayings.
(Catalogue)

For suppliants in need, to seek prophetic ritual from afar could be called *theoria*: a sacred journey undertaken as a pilgrimage, in search of spiritual insight. Seeking an archaic oracle is a model for our own *theoria* in search of Mestra, traveling in her footsteps to see what she saw and intuit what she experienced.

Travelers did not find Dodona only in myth. In search of prophetic oaks and doves, the Greek historian Herodotus wrote a description of his ancient journey to Dodona. His eyewitness account brings to life the priestesses who walked the whispering sanctuary, for he met the oak-dwellers in person, and they spoke to him there. Even more wonderful, the priestesses did not simply converse with him, but imparted the fruits of their own mytho-historical research:

> The prophetesses of Dodona say there were two black doves who flew from Thebes in Egypt... and one arrived among the priestesses in Dodona, seating herself upon an oak tree. She pronounced in a human voice that in this very place, an oracle of Zeus was to arise. Those who heard her comprehended that this was a divine message, and they carried out what the dove proclaimed. The priestesses of Dodona told me this account, the eldest of whom was named Promeneia, the second eldest, Timarete, and the youngest, Nicandra. The other people of Dodona who support and care for the shrine agreed with this story... The women who led the way in divination and served the sacred grove were called Doves." (*Herodotus, Histories*)[12]

Herodotus learned that because of a speaking dove, the priestesses of Dodona and their followers created the oracular shrine among the oaks. He preserves the sacred grove's founding legend, sprung from a bird *daimon* (or twins, or triplet doves) in a prophetic tree. He identifies the Dove priestesses as individuals, records their proper names, and respects their precedence according to age; these were honors too rarely bestowed on women of his time. These prophetesses who guarded a revered trove of esoteric knowledge trusted him to preserve their tradition; he trusted them in turn to authenticate his report. When he mentions people of Dodona who cared for the sanctuary, he is describing a local *thiasos* of worshippers who joined and sustained the Doves' oak grove rites.

When we first saw Demeter's grove in Thessaly, at the foot of the trees gushed water.

> There flowed rivulets, streams shining bright as electrum,
> through the grove the goddess Demeter loved with passion.
> (*Hymn to Demeter*)

Were such streams as prophetic as trees? In keeping with Dodona's theme of female cultic influence with a strongly allied male presence, a water nymph or naiad held sway on the site, and received worship beside Zeus and the oaks. Her name was Dione Naia.

> Dione, naiad in form, beloved of Zeus,
> ever flowing secret spring,
> your immortal liquid quenches those who thirst.
>
> Shining one, oracular,
> your lifegiving fluid wells up profound,
> murmuring beneath the oaks.

Dione Naia recalls Mestra's nymphic offerings, moistened by consecrated streams. The naiad's speaking waters surged up from oak roots, adding her liquid tones to the doves cooing in the branches above. She was an ever flowing, nurturing consort who drew seekers from afar, quenched spiritual thirst, made prophecies, soothed the brows of dusty travelers, and refreshed the heart of Zeus.

When the priestesses of Dodona interpreted divine will, they opened their minds not to some faraway invisible power, but to native trees, birds, and springs. The oracles they issued sounded through majestic oaks, shimmering water, fluttering doves, and dryads; the way souls are sometimes imagined dwelling inside bodies yet unfettered by them. In Dodona's shapeshifting tradition where nymphs were springs, trees were prophets, and priestesses were doves, those who revealed immortal wisdom spoke as diviners entranced:

> In a state of prophetic madness, not in their sound minds,
> the prophetesses of Dodona wrought wonders.
> *(Plato, Phaedrus)*

When divine ecstasy departed, so did their prophetic gift, and they did not necessarily remember what they had imparted. The message had flowed, or flown, through them. Leafy, liquid, or winged.

The Doves of Dodona are far from alone. One day Mestra herself will grow wings and fledge into flight, not only metaphorically. She will discover she can become a bird simply by having the thought. Perhaps this gift was given to her because of simple kindnesses she performed in Demeter's grove, when Mestra submerged cherished offerings in rippling streams and tucked treasures between gnarled roots. Gifts from distant days, delights for nymphs and naiads:

> a Mycenaean golden cup
> with quivering doves perched on the handles,
> or twin falcons spreading their wings.
>
> bronze statuettes of winged horses,
> sidling at the starting post, traced with silver flashing,
> muscles trembling on the edge of flight.
> *(Iliad)*

Like a winged goddess or *daimon*, birds alight and disappear into realms we cannot comprehend. Yet one day, Mestra will comprehend, from the inside. On that day, aloft on her own *theoria*, she will join Eros, Dream, Death, Delusion, Sleep, and Desire, to fly alongside prophetic Doves on the wing. Feathered Sirens know the past, the present, and all that shall ever come to be. Vulture-shaped deities eye battlefields, and human souls wing their way through the groves of the underworld. Mestra knew the Ancient Greek word for "bird" also meant "omen." She knew that the Doves were said to have been the first females on earth who ever sang their own compositions. For Mestra, the realm of bird omen will overlap into this world, and she will soar aloft beyond words or comprehension, the day she transforms and flies away free.

Longing for transformation speaks to the heart:

> It is mine to cry out with divine ecstasy,
> it is my need to range over the mountains,
> to flow across the landscape with the naiads,
> to begin a song that flies, with wings that shimmer like a
> swan.
> (*Pratinas; Homeric Hymn to Apollo*)

These are among the few words of Pratinas that have survived. They reveal that Mestra's flight from captivity into the divine landscape is what others longed for too. Who has never felt such yearning?

Shapeshifter Mestra will move freely over land and sea, the way divinities approached the realm-spanning tree of heaven:

> The goddess Hera and the *daimon* Sleep flew, light winged
> as birds,

and the tips of forest trees quivered with their passing.
Alighting on Mount Ida, the stream-watered mistress of
 beasts,
Sleep disappeared into the pine that soared the highest,
so tall that its topmost branches spanned the sunlit sky,
reaching up to touch the upper atmosphere.
inside the luxurious branches he took shelter,
in the image of a clear-singing mountain bird.
(Iliad)

Bird imagery is intuitive; it cannot be grasped. It is light and ephemeral, free as a winged creature, ever afar.

Here the Doves and dryads dance,
weaving in and out of dream,
in and out of legend,
in and out of history.

In the days when Mestra trembled to fly, myth fertilized history, and history fed myth. Some emperors too closely resembled Erysichthon. The oracle of Dodona survived until the late fourth century CE, when the shrine was forcibly closed. Then the sanctuary fell to ruin in the face of changing beliefs, the destruction of oracles, the disbandment of priesthoods, and the spreading desolation of polytheistic religious communities. By imperial order, the trees were cut down to the ground. Every single sacred oak was felled.

The Doves dwelt in their beloved forest and spoke for as long as they could.

But when at last their day of death draws near,
there rises their final dawn.

The soul shared by tree and nymph departs,
and leaves behind the light of the sun.
(Homeric Hymn to Aphrodite)

Before the end came, worship had lasted more than a thousand years among the whispering trees. Taken together, history, archaeology, cult, and myth speak of Dodona as a forest sanctuary like the one that was dear to Mestra, reminding us that such places are both imaginary and real.

I, a clear-speaking prophetess of Apollo,
am hidden beneath a stone monument in this sacred grove.
Once a maiden of gifted voice, now forever voiceless,
shackled by the fetter of hard fate.
Yet I lie here close to honored images of the Nymphs,
whose water runs down into their fountain,
and beside Hermes, statue of the grotto god, memorial in stone.
By their grace, I retain below a measure of the sovereignty I held in life.
(Pausanias)

Today, on the site of Dodona, it is said that a small tree shrine remains.[13]

Chapter 3

Oak and Axe

Who would commit sacrilege against a tree sanctuary, a consecrated grove?

The name Erysichthon means Earth-Tearer. His alternate name, Aithon, signifies someone Burning with Hunger.

We will understand Mestra more fully by understanding what she must escape: a negative father archetype of cruel greed, who kills what his daughter loves best. When she faces Erysichthon,
   Mestra is emboldened to seek her own path and discover her magical powers. But the sacred oak faces him first.
   Erysichthon exemplifies an ethical weakness that seems timeless or distinctly modern, even though ancient myths portray him in dramatic, imaginary ways. To enhance his public image, he hungered to host lavish feasts in an enlarged and renovated banquet hall, and he was determined to construct that venue at any cost. Neglecting to calculate the true price of his ambition, Erysichthon ended up enmeshed in crime, sacrificing everything, including his family and his natural environment, to his hunger for more. The power he craved involved the illusion that someone else – not him – would pay his consequences; entangled in regal delusion, he thought a sacred forest and his daughter should shoulder his debt. Specifically, Erysichthon coveted sacrosanct, forbidden lumber, regardless of what he knew about holy trees, and despite Demeter's fierce guardianship of the sacred grove she loved with immortal passion.
   August and venerated Demeter, who watches over her august and venerated oaks, is the goddess Erysichthon desecrates. It is

she who protects at all costs the divine spark within plants, the fertile force that humans pray will always spring up green.

> When Demeter, beautiful among goddesses,
> nods assent to fate, her slightest movement
> quakes the fields laden with harvests of grain.
> (*Metamorphoses*)

For her sake, life bursts forth from the cold hard seed. She coaxes the slenderest tendril to rise or stuns to stillness the hardiest root. She pours forth plentiful harvest or commands the sharp wrath of withering famine. To retaliate for the loss of Persephone – known as *Kore*, the archetypal girl – Demeter strikes the entire earth barren. Erysichthon grew up worshiping Demeter, and her budding daughter who is the maiden phase of every plant. But he fails to apply their eternal meaning to himself: to comprehend that his own daughter Mestra, beloved of Demeter, is also a *kore* to be respected; or that Demeter, the prototype of the fiercely protective mother, loves her sanctuary's trees as her own daughters.

He will not live long after daring to defy her; he will waste away to an empty husk. Here is what happened in the grove.

> When the hatchet-wielding prince and his work force shouldered in, placing profane feet on sacred soil, Demeter sensed her forest was suffering pain and was profoundly angered.
> (*Hymn to Demeter*)

To stop Erysichthon's crime, Demeter shapeshifted. She transformed herself into the persona of her priestess Nikippe and stood in his path to bar his way. Nikippe, one of Mestra's mentors, was Demeter's holy representative in the sanctuary, chosen guardian of her shrine.

Immediately Demeter likened herself to Nikippe,
holy woman respected and revered,
established by the people to be Demeter's community
    priestess.
In her hands she grasped her sacred woolen emblems and
    staff of poppy,
and from a cord over her shoulder hung the only key to the
    sacred shrine.
(Hymn to Demeter)

As Nikippe-Demeter spoke these words, she clasped holy ribbons in one hand, carried her magical poppy staff in the other, and wore her sacrosanct key of office. To disrespect a priestess in sacred regalia standing in a consecrated precinct was a terrible offense against the community, and a sacrilege against the divinity, tantamount to defying the goddess herself. (As he is in fact doing.) In disguise, Demeter speaks for the tree; she speaks for the dryad; she speaks for priestesses everywhere who must be revered; she speaks for herself, for her own holy dignity. She also speaks for Mestra, who in a fitting twist of fate, is about to find her own shapeshifting power at the brink of being destroyed by Erysichthon.

In convincing priestess form, Nikippe-Demeter calls Mestra's father to acknowledge his nurturance under the oaks, his lifelong relationship with the lifegiving grove. She encourages the aggressive leader to remember his tender childhood. As his elder, she knows him well enough to call him "child," and reminds him that he owes his very life to Demeter's mercy:

"Child, turn back your workers. Lower your axes.
You are cutting down trees who are sacred to the immortals.
Child, stay your hand, which you are raising against a
    goddess –

the goddess to whom you owe your life.
When your parents prayed for fertility in this grove under
the oaks,
Demeter heard, and so you were born, as fruitful answer to
their prayers.
Stop, or the wrath of Demeter may avenge your wrong.
You are making desolate her holy place."
(Hymn to Demeter)

But Erysichthon only escalated his violence, threatening to attack Nikippe herself:

He glared at the priestess with eyes most savage,
More fiercely than a mountain-born lion stares balefully at
a hunter.
"Back down," he growled,
"Or I will sink my great axe into your body instead."
(Hymn to Demeter)

He did not stop there. He even threatened to slay the goddess in her tree form.

"I would not care if this were the only tree Demeter loved,
or even if this oak is the incarnation of Demeter herself.
Her head with tresses of foliage is about to be struck to the
ground."
(Metamorphoses)

Why was Erysichthon doing this? The impious man tells us himself:

"These logs will put a roof on the banquet hall I am planning,
to make abundant meals to please my companions,

to feast until we are full and beyond full, forevermore, without end."
(Hymn to Demeter)

For him, his lust to preside over grand suppers staged in a refurbished banquet hall, and to eat beyond fullness with his friends, are strong enough motives to defile a sacred precinct, fell a holy grove of trees, kill a priestess, and assail a goddess. Erysichthon aspired to feast "forevermore, without end." In addition to menacing threats, his plan to gorge perpetually is blasphemy to hurl at the goddess of grain who commands invincible cycles of plenty and cessation, inevitable cycles of flush renewal and dwindling death.

The bite of the axe begins, and dreadful omens appear.

> The loftiest tree he struck first.
> Before her voice was silenced,
> she wailed a sorrowful lament to her companions.
> When his sacrilegious hand wounded her trunk,
> blood flowed forth, as when a huge bull,
> a sacrificial victim, falls before the altar,
> lifeblood pouring from the deep wound in his neck.
>
> Weakened, reeling, surrounded with ropes,
> struck by repeated blows, she fell at last,
> and the forest far and wide was shattered.
> *(Hymn to Demeter; Metamorphoses)*

Outraged, Demeter cast off her mortal shape and made a holy epiphany on earth.

> Now she appeared as the dread goddess she was,
> wrathful, terrible, and beautiful.

Her rich wheat-colored hair streamed unbound.
From her entire immortal body, a halo of light shone,
flashing bright as a bolt of lightning, illuminating the grove.
Her feet touched the earth, and her head was tall as Mount
  Olympus.
(Hymn to Demeter; Homeric Hymn to Demeter)

In this lofty form, Demeter mirrors the tree goddess behind her
in her sanctuary:

The tallest tree, mistress of the upper air, reaching to the sky,
leafy mother to all the glade, Our Lady who gathers the
  nymphs,
towering head and shoulders above the other trees.
(Hymn to Demeter)

Terror seizes the hearts of all the intruders in the grove – except
their master.

His servants almost died from fear when they beheld
  Demeter enraged.
They scattered and fled, leaving their bronze axes in the oaks.
Demeter left the workers alone, she let them go free,
for they had been helpless to disobey their harsh master's
  order.
Erysichthon commanded them to come back, threatening
  them with their lives.
He had already beheaded one of them on the spot, the one
  most true,
who had dared to speak out and had tried to stop the prince.
Deserted by his men, Erysichthon seized a hatchet himself,
  and hacked on all alone.
(Hymn to Demeter; Metamorphoses)

Stricken, the dryad spoke her final words from the heart of the tree, in human language:

"I am the dryad most beloved to Demeter,
and from the heart of her beloved tree
with my dying breath I prophecy:
punishment for this deed looms over you, Earth-Tearer,
even at this moment.
A comfort to me in my death."
(*Metamorphoses*)

Demeter added her formal curse, describing his doom.

"Since you wish to feast forever,
go ahead, you shameless glutton,
build your hall and prepare your banquets.
From this very hour, incessant feasts will be your constant concern."
(*Hymn to Demeter*)

Now that Demeter and the dryad have pronounced Erysichthon's reckoning, new allies arrive to carry out his sentence. A mountain nymph comes as a fleet messenger, along with Nemesis, the goddess of divine retribution who senses all human injustice on Earth. Demeter lends a chariot of winged dragons, who soar over mountains through the sky. All spring into action together. They summon the ruinous *daimon*, Famine:

The skeletal *daimon* flew on the wind,
crept into Erysichthon's palace under cover of night,
and entered his bedchamber, to find him helpless in sleep.
She entangled him in her embrace,
and breathed into his mouth, his throat, his chest,
casting hunger and thirst deep down, to sink into his veins.

And he began to dream of banquets,
Imagining food, and more and more food,
filled with empty cravings,
snapping his jaws,
grinding his teeth,
gnawing on barren air,
clutching and snatching at nothing.
(Metamorphoses)

Frequent feasting has arrived, in a form Erysichthon little suspects. When he wakes, he demands provisions, ceaselessly devouring everything in his sight. But nothing satiates the tree-slayer's hollow, gnawing belly.

When at last he had exhausted his family's wealth,
and had gulped down everything –
horses, birds, cattle, deer, sheep, mules, any scrap he found –
his hunger still blazed, consuming him as if he were in
    flames.
Until he turned and devoured his own limbs,
desperately consuming to the end,
feeding himself even as he disappeared.
(Metamorphoses)

The message of this consumption myth, with its grotesque conclusion, is all the clearer for being painted in bold strokes.

A warning to mortals:
avoid transgression against the gods.
(Hymn to Demeter)

Dishonor a sacred tree, and a *daimon* will avenge her. Dishonor a dryad, and the way into the enchanted grove slams shut. Dishonor Demeter, and gnawing spiritual hunger sets in.

Honor Demeter, and nature enfolds us in the protective leaves of her shimmering deep green robe. Earth unlocks the portal to the sacred: the enchanted threshold made visible, the real way through.

> The procession of our mistress,
> bathed and swathed in bridal robes.
> Never to be witnessed by the profane.
> Nymphs pour vessels to cool her lustrous limbs,
> women weave folds to drape her waist.
> Doves alight on her upraised palms,
> doves tread quivering on her shoulders.
> In one upraised palm a pomegranate,
> In the other a scepter, a golden bird alighted at the tip.
> The Graces and the Seasons entwine on her headdress.
> Her veil is sheer mist on the meadow.
> Crowned, veiled, anointed with fragrance,
> at the confluence of swelling rivers.

When we honor the sacred grove, we give life to the divinities within, and oppose the greedy values of the banquet hall. Courage is needed for the journey; we can be sure the dire story of Erysichthon's crime shocked its ancient audience. Kings and entire cities had toppled for less.

In the classical era, there was no concept of "sin" in a modern sense. Concepts of crime, sacrilege, impiety, violation, hubris, and pollution, however, did exist, and felling a sacred tree touches them all. An omen for Erysichthon, a nightmare vision:

> There were immense trees full grown,
> alder and poplar together in the glade,
> and a fir tree that reached the heavens…
> all dried up, shriveled, and long since dead.
> (*Odyssey*)

Mestra's myth foretells not only the gruesome death of one man who blindly strove to eradicate his own patron goddess's cult. It also foretells the coming destruction of the polytheistic sanctuaries of the ancient world.

> How can the impious look anyone in the face,
> and never shudder with fear – fear that the very walls,
> the wrought roof beams, the timber rafters of the house,
> or the concealing darkness they believed was their accomplice,
> set free their voice and reveal the truth?
> (*Euripides Hippolytus*)

If rafters do cry aloud, it will be with the voices of their former trees.

On that day, when news of her father's crime reached her ears, Mestra awakened to harsh reality. And she began to change. Young as she was, she was not meek or cowed. Determined and unafraid, Mestra began to weave her own devices. From this point on,

> She was crafting a strategy to outwit her father.
> (*Odyssey*)

Her co-conspirator, Demeter's sacred oak, is more potent than anything around her that chose unrootedness as a way of life. Embedded in sacred chthonic networks, oaks have always had robust access to what myth calls "revenge," through inevitable and unerring natural law. Wherever wild forces redress human imbalance on earth, all more-than-human organisms and elements have this power, granted by immortal Nemesis.

Erysichthon has not won, not even in the grove. The sentient oak's coppicing, or apparent death, does nothing to negate her divine potency, if we share her long, long view, with an eye to transfiguration. Remembering the rustic *xoanon* not to be approached with any tool, the severed trunk is still the goddess herself, immortal. Ultimately, despite appearances, the tree goddess in her sanctuary is inviolable.

Erysichthon is only a mortal holding an axe. By comparison, certain powers could survive even the blast of Zeus' thunderbolt, if the spirit was chthonic, drawing protection from deep within the earth. In Tartarus, the Titans are still alive. Typhon ripples, slumbering beneath Mount Etna, and triple bodied Geryon need only touch his mother Earth to rise mightier than ever from defeat. He only weakens when separated from her.

There is a chthonic principle of renewal post destruction who slithers through the same catalogue that preserves the Mestra fragments. She is a wily serpent. Blasted by Zeus, her soul lived on.

A serpent who in the spring of every third year
gives birth to a brood of three young snakes,
shedding her skin, lurking apart,
detests the trodden footpaths of men,
and seeks remote ridges and valleys.
When winter comes upon her, she lies underground,
in a secret chamber surrounded by her many loops and coils.

Aboveground, wintertime's frigid blasts bend majestic trees
    down to the earth,
shred beautiful leaves and petals, knock down fruit,
and swell the sea, making all things shake before its power.

You would think the serpent so 'dreadful and wild,' had
    died.
For in the dark of the year,
the thunderbolt of Zeus did overpower and destroy her.

But belowground, her soul, her psyche, survives and remains
   in the earth.
In the season of spring, when warmth returns, she rises to
   new life,
emerges from darkness into daylight,
and once again gives birth to three young.
(*Catalogue*)

The snake, whose psyche lives on, the female who survives, is
a belowground emblem of destruction and regeneration. She
curves along a slender thread of continuity against all odds,
the fragile yet invincible hidden strength of resilience. She is
a symbol of Mestra, and of the sacred life of Demeter's tree.
Driven underground, they rise renewed, resurrected manifold
in form, tripled in strength.

Is the oak prophetess of Dodona mute beneath her
monument of stone? Are cult objects thrown down to lie
submerged at the bottom of a well lifeless? Votive images
discarded and buried at the back of a cave, archaic offerings
swept from altars, or lead strips from Dodona, are not
powerless or dead. No more than the soul of a pine seedling,
sending out roots and springing up from devastation is.
Prayerful ribbons still flutter on the boughs of gnarled trees
on Mediterranean islands. The *xoanon* is perceptive; a tree
stump in the forest is not departed, but for generations shares
resources through fungal networks underground. A coppiced
oak waits then she rises multi-trunked back up to the sky.
Persephone, who like Mestra is *kore*, maiden, and daughter,
resurrects again from the underworld, and Demeter's tree
does not die into nothingness, because Demeter's mysteries
augured transformation after death.

Demeter had risen renewed from powerlessness and despair
before:

When the goddess searched for any trace of her abducted
  daughter,
her feet carried her across the world.

She crossed silver rippling, eternally flowing rivers,
to the uttermost limit where golden apples grow.
Then she sank to the earth in sorrow,
by the deep shining well of beautiful maiden dances.

She did not eat or drink,
she did not bathe her body.
A radiant goddess sat dark-cloaked,
on the dusty ground in mourning.
(Hymn to Demeter)

Yet even as she sat despondent by the well, Demeter was
devising a plan that would alter the plans of Zeus and Hades.
Neither the sky god nor his underworld brother defeated her.

There are myriad ways that consciousness remains.

*At the bread shop in the village, deciding whether to make the steep
hike up to the mysterion, the ruins of Demeter's hall of mysteries,
once more. Evenings watching the moon rise over Apollo's archaic
columns; afternoons looking at the earth anywhere in the countryside
and seeing pottery fragments from millennia scattered on the ground.
Nearby, the layered stone walls of the sanctuary of Asclepius hidden
in wild olives, brooding over the sounding ocean. Inland, the sheer
cliff where the Byzantine general rode his white stallion off the rock.
Here, the ageless marble fountain where women still gather. There,
the road curves up from the ancient harbor, beneath the brows of
temple remains: Aphrodite the Sacred and Profane; remote Hera of
the Heights. Beyond, on the curving ascent, Demeter's ancient hall*

reclines in lemon groves, in outlines still visible between the crags, broken stones tumbled in the distance.

The bakery's open doorway with its peeling green bench was swathed in the filtered shadows of a tree. Glossy leaf clusters darkened doves cooing slowly in the heat, a world away from brilliant sun beyond. It was a pomegranate tree. And there in the dappled shade a sturdy toddler stood, eating a crust of pastry, her little face, cotton dress with bright flared skirt, dusty bare feet, and tangled chestnut curls vivid in memory.

A door blown open into an ancient place, felt in the sudden gust of wind shaking branches, fluttering awnings, and ruffling the little girl's hair. Her mother and I chatted a little as the girl regarded us with solemn brown eyes. Should I climb to the mysterion that morning? Turning to go, I asked the little one's name. "to onoma tis einai Dimitra," her mother said. "Her name is Demeter."

Consciousness survived within the sentient oaks from Dodona. Like the roof beams who take voice and cry aloud:

> There was a timber taken from the sacred oaks of Dodona,
> Athena commanded to be built into the prow of the voyaging
>   Argo.
> The living beam gave the ship life,
> with the power to speak out of the storm-swept night,
> to cry out in human voice, and to issue warnings,
> retaining prophetic wisdom of her own.
> *(Apollonius of Rhodes, Voyage of Argo)*

Demeter's sanctuary, where maiden voices rang, once sheltered everything that oaks, streams, nymphs, and Mestra loved. A way of life that rustling leaves screened from view, flowing alongside private maiden rituals and devotions, born from the roots of her tree.

Lover of wilderness, let us feast on desire at the shrine of the
   goddess,
taking pleasure in the wind's warm breath upon bare
   skin.

All we need beneath our bodies is a single sheet of linen,
spread shining beneath archaic branching crowns,
on the roots of juniper or willow.
Let there be wine, and let us hear the graceful lyre of the
   Muses.
Let us drink to please our hearts.

Singing of the glorious goddess, eternal bride of Zeus,
immortal and blessed Mistress of our island.
(Athenaeus, Deipnosophists)

In the inner reaches of the forest, we will continue to find
clues to the hidden myth of Mestra, consecrated in shadows,
concealed in the branches above.

A messenger of spring is calling,
hidden among the rustling leaves,
pouring forth her song
to float above dark waters.
A trilling bird who sings honey-sweet laments,
with longing rising and falling in her voice.
(Sappho; Homeric Hymn to Pan)

The winged one sings the goddess's springtime, regeneration
for the tenderest saplings at her feet. Exploration of the sacred
grove still reveals poignant notes of hope, birds of omen for
renewal. And sacred voices raised in harmony inspire healing
remedies the world has mostly yet to explore.

Yes, in the heart of the grove she stood,
connected with all surrounding.
She had disappeared before, and now rituals of devotion,
of loss, return, and renewal, honored her willingness to
  remain,
to bear fertility for new years, new generations, new
  beginnings.
Heifer-priestess and bull priest embracing, sacrificing,
tracing steps in ritual dances tended for centuries.
Seeking her favor for this place, in her tree form of true being,
to continue her pulse through well-founded roots,
her cooling shade in the enchantment of noonday,
her combing of fierce winds to make them gentle,
her transformation of welling springs to make them sweet.

Ever and always, our inner landscapes move in everchanging
cosmic terms, and we ourselves transform:

Sorrow and joy rise and fall for all mortals,
revolving like the paths of circling constellations.
Night shimmering with stars does not forever stay.
(Women of Trachis)

A glance at what Mestra left behind.

One tradition says she cared for her father until his death, as
he begged for scraps at crossroads and wasted away. Others say
she was gone long before. Finding a mystical path of her own,
her exit stands open to possibilities and interpretations, where
she passes into the unknown.

Did she overhear what Erysichthon had done in the sacred
grove? Through the talk of women around the holy fountain?
From the murmuring oracle of a sacred spring? Inside and
outside the sanctuary, did she dread how far his transgression
would extend?

To silence Nikippe,
to fell the tree,
to make mute the dryad –
to deal with me.

Inside the echoing banquet hall sits Erysichthon, polluted by his sacrilege, transfixed.

Outside range untamed and unbound beings of many forms, including the *kore* Mestra.

If we made a map of her journey through her myth, it would lightly sketch her trails through the grove, along the shore, and across the misty ocean. But she never turned her footsteps back to the emptiness of her father's hall. It is a haunting ruin, a banquet house for no one, its portals a gateway to forest.

A tumbledown ruin hidden just beyond the tree line, screened by immense, sinewy ancient oaks. Once a private bar, now a jumble of submerged cinder block and stone with a single rusted window frame. Nature has returned; the place is barely visible beneath fern and grapevine, just a scatter of the old place for eating and drinking in the dark. Poison ivy and shrub rose are healing over all that played out in this place. Old trees spill fertile peat from their centers. Bedraggled brambles weave a painful thorn enclosure all around.

Entering more deeply into the sacred grove, we remember that wild landscapes are metaphors for our enchanted selves, dreaming in sleep and awakening, sometimes a painful awakening, to new dreams. A dark day in the sacred enclosure.

The roses shedding their leaves from garlands lay all
scattered on the ground.
(Palatine Anthology)

Yet the timber from Dodona, beloved of doves, still speaks. The tongues of ancient priestesses are still heard. We know from other myths that nymphs responded to scenes of sorrow; they came down from mountains, caverns, streams, and lakes to lament, and then planted sacred saplings all around a forest's wounds. Like the coiled serpent whose very soul Zeus thought he had destroyed, Mestra will rise in renewal. And transform.

Chapter 4

Shimmering Leaves, Dappled Mind

In her shimmering shade moved dryads,
in ribbons of flickering light,
dappled by shadow and sunbeam.
(Hymn to Demeter)

Spirits spring to life from the poetic alchemy of rooted place and mythic imagination. If we follow this flickering light, this vision of shared life for nymph and grove, dryad, and oak, we move further into the dappled shadows that naturally surround the shapeshifter. Here we glimpse how Mestra finds, as seeds and seedlings do, and waves and ripples and tidepools do, that she can transform. In the grove, Mestra comes naturally to metamorphosis, under the wing of the fluttering awareness that flourishes only in the protean shadows of primeval forest. She sees that reality itself trembles and swirls, ever inventing new spaces between elements and events, and her spirit attunes with this fluttering cosmic truth.[14]

Beloved of shimmering oak leaves, she escapes her father's curse to become radically different from a nubile girl, or the daughter of a prince who starved to death because he cut down a sacred tree. She changes because she had to change, through suffering and vulnerability. Through quivering like a tender sapling cleansed by drenching rain, growing however she can.

A tree when it is born has no predetermined number of limbs, twigs, roots, or buds. The flight of a trembling dove cannot be predicted; the ocean has no limit to its winding shorelines or infinite shapes of coiling waves. Trees, birds, and seas adapt to mutable conditions. In precisely these ways, Mestra adapts and prevails, by cherishing organic shapeshifters she knew since childhood. Reverence for ceaseless change came naturally to her, since between oaks and dryads, birds and priestesses, goddesses, and streams, all around her were metamorphosing between one another's forms.

Blessed are those who watch for birds of omen.
(*Hesiod, Works and Days*)

Archaic myth celebrates *daimones* who are never clearly nymphs and never clearly trees, but flicker in between:

In that faraway place where primeval Earth nurtures the
  most majestic trees,
they blossom, transformed through loving communion with
  the divine.
A holy fragrance drifts through the air from the peak of
  Mount Olympus,
rich in deep and fertile valleys.
The Muse of the dance gives birth to maidens there,
joined in love with the god of the river in a sacred grove.
Among the female spirits range divine winds, and there the
  lovers thrive,
as destiny counts out their long and radiant days of youth.
Their offspring move among the constellations, as immortals
  free from care.
(*Catalogue*)

A perennial question for the human *thiasos* was how to induce such a fluid spirit to attend, however fleetingly, and not to shapeshift her way through the air, across the sea, up a mountain crag, or into a subterranean spring, unheeding.

In ancient prayer, we glimpse this restless mutability:

Sacred one, you who range free over the highest mountains
    summits,
I entreat you to come close, to approach with a favorable
    spirit.
(*Theogony*)

According to primordial tradition, a vegetation goddess
quivered for flight; she cyclically departed for elsewhere, and
her whims were irresistible. Mortal rites honored her autumnal
farewells and rejoiced in her springtime returns. In advent
and departure, she did not restrict herself to a single form,
but naturally shimmered between myriad emergent forms,
flowing back and forth from wild origins. She existed in a
slow shimmer, in tree time or stone time, a wavelength slower
than tides, seasons, or circling years, too slow to be measured
in a human lifespan. Desertion was a perpetual concern, since
sometimes it seemed that a divinity had abandoned a place and
never returned.

How to invite her to cherish one place, or to inhabit one form
of being? Partly by honoring her plurality.

Who are you, Lady? Goddess, heroine, blessed immortal?
Maybe you are one of the Graces come near to us,
divine companions of the gods,
or one of the nymphs who haunt exquisite groves,
pristine mountains, river wellsprings, and lush meadows.
With your luminous sisters, you lightly range far and wide,
to attend the seeds of fertile earth and the profoundest
    depths of waters.

Shining among goddesses, hearken to my voice.
From a high mountain lookout, commanding the broad view,
I will build you an altar; I will make glorious sacrifices to
    you,

in the coming of every season.
(Homeric Hymn to Aphrodite; Theogony)

Ever many, she makes her epiphany from the mists of prehistory.

Key-Bearer, always incense rises to you,
festivals of fragrant day and torchlit processions of night.
Fine-wrought key in graceful hand,
you protect the portals that screen from common view
the wild creatures, feral trees, and writhing rivers in your
care.

To follow you is to greet the primordial mind of the forest.
You offer this hour outside time, inside shadow slant.

Worshipper, take a deep breath, and
sound the first note in her echoing hymn.
Anyone unconsecrated must depart.

Amid the swaying leaves reclines a broken wall of native
stone,
a dappled reminder before the shrine,
to humble the foot,
to stay the step.[15]

As an archaic cult title, a key-bearer served a goddess who,
paradoxically, may have dwelt in a shrine without lock, bolt,
door, or key.[16] We saw Nikippe wearing the key to Demeter's
enclosure; did it open a portal in the sanctuary's protective wall,
unlock an iron-gated shrine, or provide metaphoric meaning for
initiates as a symbol of spiritual opening? One of the tragedies of
Erysichthon's story is that he trampled over spiritual perimeters
and physical boundaries alike, without regard. In an open-air
enclosure like Demeter's, the key-bearing priestess knows the

true way in, the way to life, a secret which may or may not reflect a physical, locked entrance.

In some sacred precincts, openness and closure were signified by a seen and unseen goddess, "the goddess and the goddess behind." Many saw the former; the latter was seen by an initiated few, or even by no one.

> You are the icon seen and image concealed,
> one veiled in innermost sanctum, one open to the sky,
> one carved and one untouched.[17]

Ultimately, even in an open-air sanctuary, the *daimon* is metaphysically hidden or veiled. In the goddess,

> nature loves to hide,
> *(Heraclitus)*

transmuting into ever new guises. In linen garlands or rough bark, she is unfathomably far away, yet everywhere, and infallibly, precisely, here. She is uttermost inwardness and yet utterly distant; the epiphany of paradox, living out vows of rooted stability and radical transformation.

These are all qualities Mestra needs.

> Though perennial, the fern is – and is not the fern of last year.
> She is a Persephone, a Kore of delicate fronds.
> Not simple seed, but one who alters her form between risings,
> she is – and is not the maiden fern,
> she who fell asleep, stunned by last year's frost.

"She is – and is not" is one way to think of how Mestra is changing. There is an Ancient Greek word for fluctuating

58

revelations and concealments, shimmering mind, shifting spirit, or complex intention; a word that reflects the enchanting interplay of shadow and light, whether it appears in a forest, on the iridescent slithering scales of a dragon, or within a psyche. To the spiritual, artistic, and poetic imagination, it evokes the shimmering multiplicity of consciousness, and describes an ambience too: the mood inspired by the aura of flickering light that plays over dappled forest floors.

It is a fascinating adjective with visual and metaphorical breadth that has no English parallel. For glimpsing Mestra, it is a key-bearing word:

Poikilos (feminine *poikile*): *Something that shimmers between varieties of form, layered, complex, and enfolded in varying thoughts. A quality of Mestra's mind and body.*

A river shimmers, with willow tendrils reflected in the water. So do mosaics of aquamarine and gold, marble statues on a moonlit shore, glimmering stars, glistening skin, and lustrous tresses. Nymphs, goddesses, *daimones*, and heroines moved in a shimmer, the essence of changeability, flexibility, and unpredictability.

A quicksilver mind shimmers, one that filters out anything straightforward, drawn to glimmering realms where appearance is deceiving and meaning is never obvious. Shapeshifters had this dappled, elusive, variegated, multifaceted quality – the cunning complexity of Mestra.

What else shimmers? A sacred shrine dappled by its surrounding forest sanctuary. A heroic tomb shrouded by gardens of variegated blooms. Intricate textiles woven by the enchanted hands and complex minds of nymphs, sorceresses, goddesses, and heroines; and the curiously wrought storylines they wove around themselves too. Helen's robe. Penelope's mind. Aphrodite's intentions. Mestra's essence. All of these.

Inside Mestra are flowing forms, shifting shapes,
supple as fragrant fabric,
undulating as a wave,
as shining tapestry hung in the forest,
when a storm is coming in.

She is a story woven by women of old,
kirtle of the green lady,
sash of the gleaming moonlit goddess,
a windchime in a gale.

Orpheus with his quivering lyre originates vibration in the dead stillness of the underworld; vegetation goddesses urge buds to shiver and burst in swelling spring. Persephone descends and rises in corresponding vigor with the turning year; Artemis and the Muses make effervescent epiphanies on mountainsides, pounding pulsating rhythms with their feet. An icon illuminates a sliver of truth in flaked and gleaming gold, to flicker momentarily into life against a somber background.

In murky depths, the flash of mottled fish gills.
In dim cave shadows, the silver hand raised.
The gleam of pale feet, arched in scintillating moonlight.

These are ways reality trembles too. Now we can look afresh at Mestra, and see her as *poikile* in mind and body, fluctuating in her power to change at will.

Her flickering, flowing, and swirling between faces, voices, and imaginings also characterize Mestra's uniquely mythical and mystical companions: the shapeshifters of classical antiquity. Like her, they shimmered between forms and displayed dappled minds. We will touch on just a few who best illuminate her myth, recognizing their enchanted abilities that encompass escape, deception, defense, punishment, predation, and power.

In moments of necessity, shape changing empowered swift getaways. This was Mestra's priority when she first began to self-transform.

We already witnessed Athena do this in the *Odyssey*, when she changed herself first into a mortal advisor, then abruptly flew away as a bird. Shapeshifters often appeared so fleetingly, like the goddess Ino-Leukothea:

> Having saved Odysseus' life at sea,
> by offering him her glimmering magical veil,
> immortal Ino-Leukothea
> dove back down into the swirling sea,
> in the form of a white-plumed seabird,
> where a rippling wave obscured her
> from his sight forever.
> (*Odyssey*)

In a tight corner, threatened by adversaries, metamorphosis provided escape.

> Daphne fled pursuit, her arms sprouting leaves,
> her waist a lithe trunk, her skin smooth bark,
> a laurel tree with whispering branches.

> Arethusa sprang away, evading a close chase,
> her feet now flowing, her ringlets rippling down cool,
> her supple form a spring of gushing water.
> (*Metamorphoses*)

Such urgent escapes, paramount for Mestra, signaled female victimization, and provided a mythic outlet for rare and valuable cultural critique.

We met the goddess Nemesis before, when she came to Demeter's aid in the grove. A shapeshifter herself, Nemesis not only punished human wrongdoing; she had suffered profound divine injustice too.

> Nemesis bore a child to the king of the gods,
> by force, overpowered by Zeus's violent strength,
> feeling shame and righteous anger in her heart.
> She fled through seas and oceans as a fish,
> she fled to the ends of the earth as every kind of wild beast,
> shapeshifting in flight, trying to escape her pursuer.
> (Cypria)

To expose shapeshifting legends of pursuit and violence, forthright Arachne wove into her *poikile* narrative tapestry a series of tragic female metamorphoses, when immortal gods deceived mortal females.

> There was Europa, abducted by Zeus in the likeness of a bull,
> Asterie, gripped by the wrestling claws of Zeus as an eagle,
> Leda, subdued beneath Zeus' wings when he was a swan.
> Zeus put on a golden disguise for Danae,
> and approached Persephone as a striped snake.
> Poseidon the most expert shapeshifter,
> came to maidens as a bull, a river, or ram;
> a stallion to Demeter, a winged bird to Medusa, a dolphin to
>   Melantho.
> Apollo used metamorphosis too, to come upon virgins as a
>   rustic peasant,
> a bird of prey, or a rugged lion.

Such were the crimes of shapeshifting gods,
and Arachne wove their stories.
(*Metamorphoses*)

Arachne's subsequent fate shows that the power Mestra was acquiring could be severe, when metamorphosis was meted out as trial or punishment:

A spider now, Arachne still spins, by Athena's unalterable
decree.
Arachne's crime was telling the truth.
Artemis's wrath made Actaeon a stag, torn apart by his own
hounds.
Circe is prowled around by lions, wolves, and boars,
beasts who were once men.
Sailors who dared offend Dionysus, attempting to sell him
as a slave,
swim as dolphins forever.

Shapeshifting could be terrifying, as when an unwelcome suitor displayed his potency to the maiden he sought to win.

While I still lived in the halls of my father,
I had the most painful reluctance to marry,
because my suitor was the god of all rivers that flow on earth.
He demanded my hand from my father,
appearing in three distinct forms: a bull,
a wily dragon with swiftly sliding coils,
and the body of a man with the face of a bull.
From his bushy beard torrents gushed forth,
like drenching streams spurting from a fountain.
In utter terror of such a suitor, of being taken to his bed,
my every prayer was for death.
(*Women of Trachis*)

Overwhelming outpourings of emotion could alter physical form:

> Grief for her children poured down in waterfalls of tears,
> the face of stone, the lonesome fountain of mourning
> that once had been Niobe.

> Weeping for her daughter,
> the cries of Alkyone became the lilting call of a sea bird,
> forever searching over the waves.
> (*Iliad*)

Yet metamorphosis could be a reward. Baucis and Philemon humbly cherished and tended a sacred landscape for many years until old age. For their loving service to the sanctuary, at their moment of death they were transformed into mutually loving trees.

> They shade their beloved temple, two bodies entwined in
>   twin trees,
> oak and linden together, interleaved in branching embrace.
> (*Metamorphoses*)

Most enigmatically, shapeshifting was the practice of elusive polymorphs, who via transformation expressed their inherent mutability, freedom from constraint, and existence beyond categorization. Such metamorphic skill overwhelmed opponents and gained adroit advantage. These techniques bring us closer to Mestra.

> When you try your strength to keep a forceful grip on
>   Proteus,
> Ancient Man of the Sea, prophet whose wisdom knows all
>   depths,

through your hands flow forms that writhe to escape:
roaring walrus, shaggy boar, scaly dragon –
any animal that creeps over the earth –
ebbing salt water, or divinely kindled fire.
(Odyssey; Vergil, Georgics)

Periklymenos, favored by Poseidon
to become more forms than could ever be named,
shifted into many shapes to defend his city against Heracles.
He perched on Heracles' chariot in the fierce form of a raptor,
making ready to fight the hero with his wiles.
(Catalogue)

Nereus, a man above and a fish below,
unerringly wise and forthright in prophecy,
swims among his hundred lovely-haired sea nymph
     daughters,
and rises in any shape he desires,
from echoing silver caverns of the teeming Aegean sea.
(Iliad, Theogony)

Tiresias, the powerful seer, living through seven generations
     of humankind,
was sighted then blind, dreadfully harmed, and deeply
     favored by goddesses.
When he saw two serpents mating on mount Cithaeron,
he picked up the female and suddenly took on a female form.
He lifted the male and returned to a male shape once more.
Then he knew the past and future, and flawlessly interpreted
     divine signs.
In death Persephone granted him to retain his prophetic
     mind below the earth,
steadfast in full consciousness, while other souls fly
     aimlessly, thin as wisps of smoke.

(Hesiod, Melampodia; Callimachus, Hymn on the Bath of Pallas; Odyssey)

Among these adepts, Thetis surfaces again in Mestra's sphere. She is akin to Mestra because she is a virginal shapeshifter who transmutes herself to flee marriage, and because she crafts intrigues where her cunning must stay submerged and concealed:

> Who could hold onto a snarling leopardess,
> fetter a gush of water, or subdue a spurting fountain?
> Under attack, Thetis writhes away from embrace –
> and then arches her silver leap, plunging into the waves.
> *(Metamorphoses)*

Ino-Leukothea rematerializes in Mestra's sphere too, for just as Mestra is destined to do, she transcended mortal limits in her newfound marine element.

> Slender-ankled Ino transformed into a sea bird,
> she who was called Ino in life, but now is Leukothea the
>   ageless,
> a mortal shapeshifter who took immortal form.
> Once upon a time she spoke on earth with human voice,
> but now by fate she is worshiped among goddesses in the
>   depths of the salty sea.
> *(Odyssey)*

If we follow Ino-Leukothea down into the depths, we discover that after nursing the infant Dionysus she was transfigured from a mortal maiden to a goddess of the sea, a rescuer of drowning sailors accompanied by triple maenads, directing Dionysian mysteries.

All these changed and changeable beings, who have inspired spiritual and mythological contemplation for millennia, illuminate something profound about Mestra. Contemplating their transmutations between forms, we contemplate Mestra afresh, in whom their embodiments intertwine. She endured, escaped, survived, grew wiser with each transformation, and eventually achieved transcendence in the sea. All along, her *poikile* cleverness flowed in dappled, swirling forms.

Shafts of streaming sunlight dance between mist-fine robes of rain. Wherever streams drip gently from shadowed rock, and moist plants drape in delicate fringe, to the ancient mind these folds evoked the female. Gown, bosom, lap, womb, soft nesting hollow; all were harbors of refuge. Metamorphosis illuminates the layered consciousness of forest: honeybees awash in hive mind encircle beeches who foster young from curvaceous roots. The oblique tactic of an ancient heroine might move like an olive tree, whose silver bark has flowed around a rusted gate, transmuting harshness in swirling veils of bark. From such transformation, once initiation begins, there is no turning back.

She is on her way. When we catch sight of shimmering Mestra, we glimpse vibrant life inside and around her, flowing between forms.

May ever-shifting versions of her continue to arise in our dappled minds.

O *kore* of shimmering manifestation,
come from private gardens and speaking springs,
in the rustle of oak leaves,
the flutter of doves,
in the sounding sea.
Come to us with kindly heart,
and depart whenever you will.

Still she ranges shore and grove, and to the reverent may appear
in the shape of anything, anything at all.

A delicate skill. She will need it.

> Sapling loosening verdant tresses, silver cascade of rippling
>   limbs,
> lifting wrists of swirling stems, expressive in the dance.

> Ankle-roots in the rain, robed in leaves of linen, she shimmers.

> Maiden or tree? Tree or maiden?
> In moonlight, irresistible.

Chapter 5

The Image of a Virgin

Being irresistible, for many a maiden in many a myth, becomes a double-edged sword. It goes that way for Mestra.

> She is a wonder for mortals to behold,
> courted by all the men of property in the region,
> who propose to marry her and take her to wife.
> (*Odyssey*)

What are the suitors falling for? Not only for her father's ruse.

> Longing overcomes them, Eros melts their hearts,
> and they pray to lie beside her, mingled in a loving bed of
>   marriage.
> (*Odyssey*)

Being a desire just beyond reach may sound romantic. But that is not how Mestra experienced the arrival of her suitors. Now she threads her way through danger and sharpens skills for narrow escapes, in and out of a perilous household that is imperial yet impoverished.

As we already know, Mestra's name means Clever or Cunning. She has another name too. Later traditions call her Hypermestra, suggesting new facets of her story. Where today we might talk of someone so appealing that they "turn heads," her alternate name suggests multiple courtships, conjuring up the image of a woman so memorable, so unforgettable, that she "turns minds." Beholding her inspires men to turn their thoughts to marriage, to hold her in memory and hope. Taken all together, her names paint the image of a *kore* possessing complex and remarkable intelligence, who is extraordinarily, multiply, wooed.

When a crisis in a rite of passage opened the portal for her metamorphoses to begin, the imminent threat was marriage.

> Erysichthon had nothing left now except his daughter.
> Finding she had the power to change her form,
> he betrayed her trust, sold her, and handed her over for money,
> as often as he could to different masters.
> But she escaped, changing from mare to bird to ox to stag,
> and with each new fraud, her father got more provisions for his appetite.
> (*Metamorphoses*)

Once he depletes the palace treasury and spends his dynasty's wealth for piles of food to fill his empty stomach, Erysichthon brokers betrothals and swindles prospective grooms. For him, a daughter is currency, just as trees are lumber to be used.

To highlight his underhand dealing, Mestra's myth purposely creates ambiguity between betrothal and sale, groom and master, marriage, and ownership. Confusion between roles was easy to stir up because marriage in this archaic Greek context meant the formal exchange of wealth for a bride.

> In days of old, men who courted a woman of noble birth,
> the daughter of a wealthy father, strove to compete with one another.
> They brought in fat cattle and fleecy sheep to feast the family of the bride,
> and offered glorious gifts.
> (*Odyssey*)

Exchange of resources created the social framework for producing legitimate offspring, along with the theoretically permanent transfer of the bride to the groom's ancestral home. Fathers attempting to secure heirs arranged such transactions, to continue their line of descent. If the maiden cooperated, they hoped to procure a fertile lineage. Early marriage formulas specified the production of legitimate children as the purpose of marriage, and the *Catalogue* explicitly notes why one of Mestra's suitors wooed her:

> So that from Mestra his seed (*sperma*) would endure among humankind.

Social protocols, tightly fused with biological goals, made marriage a potentially treacherous passage. In myriad ancient myths:

> The girl like a tender plant
> grows in the place she knows.
> Harsh sun, rain, and wind do not confound her, for she is
>   sheltered.
> Free from care, she leads her life with pleasure,
> until the day she is no longer called maiden,
> but a woman and a wedded wife.
> Then her countless troubles begin.
> (*Women of Trachis*)

What was it like to be valued so little while being valued so much?

> The gentle girl with pitiful eyes
> sat on a hillside as far away as she could,
> waiting for the outcome,

for the winner to be declared her husband.
She looked on in silence,
while the struggle seethed around her.

And then, like a calf that is lost from the fold,
she was gone from her mother.
(Women of Trachis)

Is Mestra gone from her mother? Amid all this bartering and struggling, while the bride is going to the highest bidder, her mother is notably absent. The myth of Persephone's abduction displayed the negative consequences of Father Zeus not involving Mother Demeter in marital negotiations; this may well have been the case with Mestra too. In the face of Erysichthon's shameful hubris, his wife seems to have provided Mestra with temporary refuge, a place to work beside her at the loom, yet remained powerless in her daughter's dilemmas. Whether by force or by choice, Mestra's mother complied with Erysichthon's schemes and helped cover up his crimes.

Yet in dark corners his devouring secret grew.
(Hymn to Demeter)

Trying to maintain a tottering palace, Mestra's mother stands overshadowed, nameless, in her own silent tragedy behind her husband. Mestra is orphaned, though both her parents are alive.
She could have been frightened.

Like a shy fawn born only days ago,
left by her mother in remote mountains,
who quivers with terror at every forest breeze.
(Anacreon; Horace)

But Mestra didn't hesitate. Maybe she wasn't frightened at all. There is more than one way to be like an animal.

> Once she got free, she darted away swift as a doe,
> and came back to the halls of her father,
> transforming herself back into a woman,
> though someone would come to lead her away once more.
> (Catalogue)

Again and again, she finds trapdoors and secret exits out of her father's halls, out of marriage that was meant to be a one-way passage.

On one of her escapes, she encountered the god Poseidon (the subject of the next chapter). At this point, she is disheveled and reduced to wearing ragged clothes, signs of her supposed low value and her father's disregard. As Ovid said, "Mestra was worthy of a far better parent." Her pursuer is hard on her heels, and she is desperate. She calls for and receives Poseidon's help:

> When her father sold her, she refused.
> Stretching out her arms, her palms above the water,
> she prayed for Poseidon to save her from slavery.
> Poseidon heard and answered her prayer.
> He gave her a masculine form and features,
> with all new clothes and gear.
> She looked just like a fisherman.
> (Metamorphoses)

Her tracker came to the seaside looking for her, but he saw nobody except a young man calmly fishing. Deep irony colors the scene, while fisherman-Mestra dangles a hook and line in front of a pursuer who is trying to hook her. He claims that he is missing a slave girl who she belongs to him and asks fisherman-Mestra for assistance – in catching herself. As a fisherman, Mestra engages her latest master-purchaser-groom in deft and friendly chat, including a false oath by the god responsible for her disguise.

"Have you seen a slave girl, wearing shabby clothes, with dirty hair?" he asked. "She belongs to me." Then he went further:

> "Fisherman, I wish you a tranquil sea,
> where gullible fish never suspect a hook
> until they are caught and done for. By the way,
> can you tell me where the girl has gone,
> who I saw standing on the shore just now?
> Her footsteps stop right here, beside you."

Who is the gullible fish? Relieved, fisherman-Mestra rejoiced that she was being asked to track herself down, and smoothly replied:

> "I would be happy to help you.
> But I swear by the artful mind of the god Poseidon,
> that all the long while I've been fishing on this shore,
> I have seen no females here.
> No one else has been by the water. Just me."
> *(Metamorphoses)*

"He" is telling the truth, technically anyway. Her tracker goes away empty-handed. On the seashore Mestra appears in trickster mode, reveling in the chance to walk free along the beach as a male, expressing freedoms a girl might only dream of. For the moment with her fishing line, hunted as she is, she is enjoying winning the game. It turns out crafty speech, as surely as beauty and wit, is among her notable features. But Mestra has not really escaped. Her father has learned her secret.

Nonchalance aside, in each metamorphosis, she simply must succeed, for this is not a game. Other myths tell the tale. Herakles killed the shapeshifter Periklymenos when he suddenly saw through his cunning bird disguise. The risk described by a river god, who was mutilated when he lost a wrestling contest with Heracles, shows what is at stake if a shapeshifter is ever caught:

> "He seized me by my neck and flung me to the earth.
> Inferior in muscle, I turned to guile.
> I transformed into a gigantic looping serpent,
> slippery with venom, and I coiled around him hissing.
> But he recognized me despite my skill, and jeered:
> 'What good is that precarious disguise of yours?
> Borrowed skin will not save you; I have seen through you,
>   false snake.'"
> (*Metamorphoses*)

With each betrothal, the river god's solution was also Mestra's:

Inferior in muscle, she turned to guile.

Among the suitors who sought Mestra's hand (and son-in-law status in the royal house), most are unnamed. But they were numerous. Like Helen in her lovely veils, Penelope in her well-built palace, or swift-footed Atalanta winning every race, Mestra was developing her own catalogue. Of suitors.

Each was rejected in turn. Some who came courting, however, were more challenging than others. Two were serious contestants, because they aligned with Mestra's most memorable quality: each was legendary for conniving tricks. Their names were Sisyphus and Autolycus.

First came wily Sisyphus: archetypal trickster, cheater of death, and enemy of Zeus. Sisyphus swindled Hades out of his own funeral rites, bound up the *daimon* Death, and made a daring escape back into the upperworld. He is most famous now as the soul in the underworld who for his crimes eternally rolls a boulder up a hill, a massive rock that endlessly slips back down again. While he was alive, Sisyphus approached Mestra's father to negotiate not for himself, but for his son Glaucus.

> He meant to escort home the quick-glancing, lovely-cheeked
> girl,
> as a wife to please his son's heart.
> *(Catalogue)*

But Mestra won't have him. Right outside the wedding chamber, she took on forms of her own choosing.

> A filly rolling the whites of her eyes at the bridal bridle,
> bucking, kicking sharp heels at anyone
> foolhardy enough to venture near.

> They ran and got a rope and halter,
> but she became a lowing heifer,
> deafening the groomsmen,
> her neck too muscular for slim cords to secure.

> They found a weighty yoke,
> to bend her neck to marriage,
> but now she was a stag,
> brandishing sharp antlers,
> overleaping the fence with effortless strength.

> Looking back, she stood a moment poised,
> calmy regarding would-be captors.

Then she ran away on swift hooves. It was not the wedding anyone had in mind.

Immediately, strife and dispute arose between Sisyphus and
  Erysichthon,
over the slim-ankled girl.
(Catalogue)

Their quarrel is about a man trying to secure a manageable
wife for his son. For his genealogy, in fact. Female misbehavior
adversely affected male prestige:

Make sure you marry a chaste maiden,
so that you can teach her trustworthy ways.
Carefully look all around her situation,
making sure you don't become a fool in front of your
  neighbors.
(Works and Days)

To restrain Mestra, they resorted to chains. It didn't work.

Orders were issued:
she was bound with powerful fetters, under guard.
Even still, she freed herself and dashed away,
for no one realized yet that she could shapeshift.

A temporary respite only.
Sisyphus was gaining ground.
Found working at home by her mother's loom,
she was forced back out again.
(Catalogue)

When she shapeshifted to elude Sisyphus, Mestra outwitted one
of the most notorious tricksters of all time.

Mestra deceived one who was very clever,
Sisyphus, whose mind exceeded all other men's.

Yet the girl with the glancing eyes and expressive face
    outfoxed him,
after he promised an extravagant bride price:
a hundred mane-tossing stallions,
whole herds of lowing oxen,
flocks and flocks of fleecy sheep and shaggy goats,
payment promised and received.
(Catalogue)

Sisyphus's catalogue of bridal gifts sounds uncomfortably familiar. Some of the animals on offer – breed stock to secure breed stock – were beings she became. To her, the list of animals sounded like a list of resourceful allies. Not herds but individuals, models for metamorphoses, shapes she inhabited and understood from the inside. But to ravenous Erysichthon, the bride-price list of gifts on hoof sounded like a savory menu. Somehow it becomes impossible not to think of the Titan Cronus, the prototype of the father who devours his own young.

In an alternative version of Mestra tricking the trickster, it was the master criminal Autolycus who came wooing. She was called the wife of this fabled thief, who had a metamorphic specialty of his own. He could transform stolen goods to make them unrecognizable:

Whatever he took into his hands,
he could change the appearance of all of it, or even make it
    invisible.
(Catalogue)

Like Sisyphus in disposition,

Autolycus excelled all men in artful thievery and slipping
    out of sworn oaths.
(Odyssey)

Autolycus, a character wisely viewed with suspicion by those he chanced to meet, stole precious heirlooms and entire herds of cattle. From his father Hermes he attained the stature of hero and received the gift of escaping all capture. These honors explain why his name was linked with Mestra's, though she used metamorphic craft and slippery words not to steal, but to gain her freedom and outwit her father's embezzling schemes. If we put Autolycus and Sisyphus, two like-minded rivals, side by side to vie with one another in all their deceitful arts (and legend says they did compete), artful Mestra stands in the picture between these figures of fabled cunning. In courtship they competed for her; in shrewdness they competed against her.

Yes, she could become a mare or heifer, but mares and heifers went as bridal presents. For winners of masculine athletic contests, these animals stood as prizes. So did women.

> The prizes are in place and await the competitors:
> golden cauldrons, bronze tripods, grey iron,
> horses, mules, droves of sturdy cattle,
> and fair-girdled women.
> First place: a woman skilled in flawless weaving, to be led
>   away by the winner.
> Second place: a six-year-old mare, unbroken and pregnant
>   with young.
> (*Iliad*)

Why were Sisyphus and Autolycus so eager to win Mestra? I wonder if, unlike ordinary men, these two thieves admired her arts of deception, which surpassed their own skills. Self-shapeshifting was beyond their repertoire of cunning tricks, even though Autolycus could transform the loot he stole. His name did mean The Wolf Himself, suggesting he appreciated wolfish ways. For as long as the marriage to Autolycus lasted, Mestra found empathy for her animalistic powers, and was daughter-in-law to quicksilver Hermes, god of all tricksters. But how long did she stay? When Autolycus chose her for his wife and Sisyphus strove to acquire her for his son, both were trying to hold onto one who slipped away from the fame of their legendary misdeeds, out into her own story. In the end, anyone who tries to hold on to a shapeshifter must let go.

On the loose, Mestra was partly enticing, partly trouble: living dangerously, evading captors, and acquiring shady company. We know her suitors were indignant.

Penelope's mob of admirers complained when she crafted effective devices against marrying any of them, and the same grievances could be made against wily Mestra:

> She is exceedingly resourceful; her cleverness has won her
>   renown.
> Her thoughts are filled with unheard-of wisdom.
> Yet she makes one repeated mistake: refusing marriage.
> Some *daimon* must have given her this strategy.
> Does she have some secret plan in her heart?
> Is she weaving some plot of her own?
> She should stop being so ingenious.
> She should stop making her fame so bright.
> Let her yield, and accept a husband properly:
> a man who is one of us.
> (*Odyssey*)

Female freedom thwarted male plans and grumbling ensued. As the forge god Hephaestus complained when he was irate with wandering Aphrodite,

> Her father should refund to me the entire bride-price,
>   as much as I handed over on account of his shameless
>   daughter.

She is beautiful but does not control her impulses.
(Odyssey)

Like Aphrodite, Mestra did not sit timidly by. Nor did she, any more than Aphrodite ever did, listen to protests. She was a *kore* living out a radical strategy of female disobedience.

Half nymph
with glancing eyes, fair of face, and
half monstrous snake: dreadful, terrifying, huge.

Well, not really.

Half nymph,
with glancing eyes, fair of face, and
half serpent whenever she wanted to be.
A metamorphic mystery.
(Theogony)

Part of Mestra's metamorphic mystery lay in a surprising direction. Once her marriageability or ownership was contested, the mystery was her virginity, which became notorious by being undefined. Artful in this domain, and clever beyond categorization, she employed her maidenly state as a smokescreen, mystifying suitors, grooms, husbands, masters, and captors, by technically remaining virginal no matter how many weddings she had.

Fortunately for Mestra, *parthenos* or "virgin," was more a social grouping than a sexual status for females in archaic Greece. *Parthenos* signified an unwed girl, one who had never borne a child. It described a stage of life: the springtime of a young woman's unfettered, budding vitality, vibrant with the promise of approaching womanhood.

While seemingly submitting to betrothals or even weddings, Mestra's mystique of self-transformation left her *parthenos* status indefinable – unbound and untethered – since any prevailing definition for a mortal girl could not suit a shapeshifter. She became, in fact, a *poikile* virgin.

Sitting within the folded lap of a long-ago coppiced oak, the darkling original stump, and her sapling generations rising from the same stem. Serpent-rooted oak arms have lifted this low throne in the meadow. Here is heard the poikile speech of tree, where each meaning is a constellation, root ball, spiderweb, leaf vein, or fungus whorl. Here reality and myth spiral together, moving in feeder root metaphors. This oak is decomposing with age and newborn with young. Fitting no known category, she is – and is not – parthenos.

The very first created woman in Greek myth was also an enigmatic creature with an undefined quality of virginity. She was Pandora, the prototypical female, who appeared "in the likeness of a modest and chaste virgin."

> Hephaestus the craftsman took clay, and through the will of
>   Zeus,
> shaped a wondrous thing to behold:
> Pandora, the first woman.
> She was the likeness of a modest and chaste virgin,
> with a face as lovely as a goddess,
> speaking with human will and voice.
> She was endowed with womanly arts and *poikile* weaving,
> adorned in shining garments and lovely garlands, all
>   Athena's gifts.
> Aphrodite poured the radiance of the Graces around her
>   face,
> and instilled in her the power of desire,
> passion that brings pain and saps men's strength.

Hephaestus fashioned her a cryptic crown of gold,
intricate and peculiar, carved with all the life and voice of
every wild beast born on land and sea.
Immortals and mortals alike were astonished to see her:
this lovely evil, this unmanageable trick.
She had the shameless mind of a temptress, knew flattering
    words,
and had beguiling, thieving ways.
She was destined to bring trouble to men.
Yet there she stood: the very image of a shy and modest
    maiden.
(*Theogony; Works and Days*)

Every dreaded beast on land and sea contrived to caper on Pandora's peculiar crown; all creatures *parthenos* Mestra could become. Were Pandora and Mestra chaste – or clever about contriving their chaste images, concealing keen minds and oblique intentions inside their captivating appeal? Appearing virginal could be a female form of self-preservation. Myth tells of fathers who threw their daughters over cliffs for premarital amours.

And yet – the shameless mind of a temptress? With beguiling, thievish ways? Timeworn accusations. A shape-changing femme fatale, a betrothed *parthenos* who snapped her tether and ran free, like Pandora with her unmanageable allure and intricate designs, raised patriarchs' anxieties to new heights. In animal terms, Mestra on the loose is a stray, beyond a father's or husband's restraint. What to do about modest-seeming maidens so guilelessly appealing, yet so dangerously uncontrolled, and so reputedly sly?

In narrow-minded interpretations, Mestra has been labeled a devious, promiscuous woman or a prostitute, since there wasn't supposed to be any such thing as a serial bride. Clearly, in keeping with suspicions about Pandora and women in general, responsibility for Erysichthon's fraud has been firmly transferred onto Mestra's shoulders. How far did Mestra get into those wedding nights anyway? As far as the bridal chamber? Did she flee to prevent consummation, or slip out the following dawn? And aren't those prurient questions? Her indecent sales or multiple weddings scandalized later moralizers who promoted a pseudo-medical definition of virginity. For some, a shapeshifting *parthenos* in all her complexity sounded uncomfortably close to just plain shifty. From a wider point of view, blaming her raises questions about female agency, and even personhood.

While we are asking questions about suspicions, however, let's go ahead and ask a useful one. Was Mestra really a sorceress? The word here for a female adept, *pharmakis*, seems to be a placeholder for a woman incomprehensibly knowledgeable and unconventional, a riddle who fits no "normal" behavior for femininity. Escaping any conventional, obedient role, Mestra is essentially being called a wisewoman or witch skilled at herbs, drugs, and poisons, to try somehow to explain her uncanny ability. She does not seem to have been a sorceress, or to have used plants in those ways. But at the very least, it is intriguing that an ancient commentator chose this term to try to classify a female who defied classification; suggesting awareness of women, daimones, and heroines (like Helen, Circe, or Medea) who did possess magical skill with plants and lived esoteric or liminal lives. A *pharmakis* moved among mysterious women who would have befriended and understood a shapeshifter.

Myth explores many pathways, including wish fulfillment. No wonder Mestra sheds mortal morality to become a transformative *daimon*. Whether she appears winged, hooved, or in full fishing gear, she bewitches many a suitor. She is a thought-provoking paradigm of radical self-transformation who leaves rules and rule makers, such as they were, unmasked and open to question.

Enough of labels placed on women,
enough of men and contests of wealth,
of oxen and goats and sheep – and asses.
Let's turn this around and look at it from her perspective.

As she sketched out her next escape, who were Mestra's transformative paradigms?

Musing on a plot of her own, she looked to the divine. Thought-provoking goddesses sprang to mind, those who enjoyed absolute freedom to come and go at will. Willfully making epiphany and departing, renewing their forms, and rejuvenating their virginity, tree and vegetation goddesses showed Mestra the way.

After her restorative bath in the sea each spring, a tree goddess replenished her maiden season when she returned to her sacred forest. Persephone rose as a maiden annually from the wintry embrace of Hades. Aphrodite was bathed for renewal by the Graces before she returned as a perpetual bride to her temple. Seasonally, Artemis, Athena, and Hera were reestablished as virgins in sacred groves. Each re-emerged as *parthenos*.

Since the goddess's first primordial spring,
fertility and chastity meet in the forest.

As for Mestra, for whom fertility and chastity meet in the oak,

Someone brings her a glistening gown, but it is not the short mantle of sacred grove, light for darting over meadow and mountain, racing with the wind. Someone bestows an elaborate belt, but these are not the tassels of nymphs. Someone contributes a gleaming veil, and someone

cools her brow with fragrant water, bridal lustrations. But these are not the homespun scarves of the oak or the salt-fresh bath of the sea. Some drape her hair with ribbons, where once the dryads wreathed fresh flowers. Gentle hands provide elaborate touches to her costume. They are not the hands she longs for.

In the end, ingenue or prostitute, wife or bride are categories that pale beside Mestra's colorful range of transformations. Her maidenly vigor, like her body and mind, is *poikile*. She is enticing yet suddenly vanishes, embodying the eternally far-off quality of sacred grove or wild creature.

Under modest veil, she glances sideways,
ponders becoming anything, anything she imagines.

Failing at a female rite of passage such as marriage, childbirth, or coming of age – as Mestra is purposely failing – most often brought dire consequences. But we know from myth and cult alike that failure created heroines. Only those who had stumbled knew how rocky the path was. In preparation for marriage, young hopefuls climbed up to the sanctuaries of uncanny goddesses, nymphs, and heroines, who dwelt outside the rule, to worship them and to seek their mercy as numinous guides.

I am coming to the beloved sanctuary of shining goddesses,
ascending, leaving behind the walls of mortal habitation,
and I bear an offering in my hands: a pair of sweet
   pomegranates.
I am coming to pray to the lovely flowing streams,
that I may accomplish a desirable union in marriage,
experience the works of Eros that are dearest to women and
   men,
and find a firmly rooted bed of love.
(Alcman)

Prayers and sweet pomegranates may beckon in Mestra's future. At this moment in her story, however, she is caught betwixt and between.

Each faltering rocky step, every venture out onto the seashore, or into the depth of a grove, is divination: a surrender to wisdom beyond her own. A willingness to place feet where they are called and accept the outcome. In accordance with ancient practice, providing an opening for the fates.

At this juncture, fleeing from one failed nuptial rite to another, Mestra also turned for inspiration to the myth of Iphigeneia, who was transformed by Artemis at the altar of her wedding. While Erysichthon craved food, Iphigeneia's father Agamemnon coveted a favorable wind so his fleet could sail to the conquest of Troy. Mestra and Iphigeneia both invoke metamorphosis as liberation, from a parent who is willing to destroy the feminine for his own advantage. Iphigeneia's plight dramatizes the mythic motif of the negative father in vivid extremity:

> Her father hardened his heart, to sacrifice Iphigeneia for his war.
> Bound and silenced, trussed in her bridal veils,
> her eyes sent pleas for pity to her unheeding captors.
> The *kore* they had known, lovely in song and dance,
> brought here to die in ceremony as bride.
> (Aeschylus, *Agamemnon*)

According to some versions, Iphigeneia perished at the hand of Agamemnon. In other endings, Artemis metamorphosed Iphigeneia in the nick of time, foiling the wedding party's savage plot. Iphigeneia was not a shapeshifter. But like Mestra, she embodies the themes of virginal flight from the captivity of marriage, destructive father of a *parthenos*, and marriage-as-death for brides.

To rescue a bride in danger, Artemis could effortlessly metamorphose her into an animal or whisk her far away. In the case of Iphigeneia, one esoteric tradition said Artemis changed her into an avatar of the triple goddess Hekate:

> Iphigeneia did not die, but by the judgment of Artemis, became Hekate.
> (*Catalogue*)

Others claimed Artemis swept Iphigeneia far away to an exotic land to be a priestess in her cult.

The goddess whisking a bride away to safety is an accomplishment Mestra learns for herself when she transforms her own body into a wild beast or deer who darted lightly away.

> To dance beneath twisted mountain junipers,
> in a lonely place for Artemis mistress of animals,
> as she-bear, she-wolf, or trembling hare,
> never to be tamed, racing with the wind,
> bridle-loosener, filly-hearted, windy-hooved,
> too nimble in body, too agile in mind, to fasten the yoke of
> marriage.

Mestra, the image of a virgin, the paragon of a much-courted maiden, many times sold, and many times redeemed, also approached the bridal altar, apparently obeying – then in a bold mythic twist, she leapt away wild. May Iphigeneia have done so too, through the power of Artemis the Loosener of Bonds?

A wild cherry tree leans precariously above the brook, shooting buds straight up from her tipping point, with stems spontaneously surging from the base where a branch has snapped. These buds were dormant,

invisible under the bark until the moment of peril, and then up leapt
a smooth green stem out of scaly textured brown. Epicormic genesis.
Not an original branching, a later burgeoning by necessity. From
fracture arise forms unforeseen.

Mestra, *parthenos* in forms unforeseen, has loosened her bonds,
left behind the walls of mortal habitation, fled the palace,
and eluded her father's plot, rejecting the ruler for whom
consumption is all. As fugitive bride, she has picked all the
locks, slipped out of all the bridal chambers, and failed to find a
firmly rooted bed of love. Now she stands poised on a precipice.

> By the echoing shore of the grey and misty sea, gazing over
> the infinite water.
> (*Iliad*)

Looking out to sea, was she dreaming of Pandora, Persephone,
Thetis, Iphigeneia? Or maybe Ino-Leukothea, whom we met as
Odysseus' winged savior, the sea bird goddess with the magic
veil? Legends spoke of women like Ino-Leukothea, who leapt
from cliffs into the teeming depths and rose transformed into
shining goddesses or weeping seabirds, tragic heroines passing
into divinity. But Mestra doesn't leap. Something else begins to
happen.

As Mestra gazed outward, the Sea began to gaze back.

Chapter 6

Over the Wine-Dark Sea

Earthquake of earth and storm of sea,
lord of vast ocean, gulfs, and promontories,
Earth-shaker, twofold is your divine gift:
to be tamer of sacred horses with whitecap flowing manes,
and protector of ships who cross you at their peril.
Hail, Poseidon, dark one who holds the earth in your cupped
    hand.
Keep a compassionate heart, immortal.
Come to the salvation of sailors when they are in mortal
    danger.
(Homeric Hymn to Poseidon)

The lover Mestra chose at last surpassed any hero or mortal suitor, for he was the brother of Zeus and Hades, an immortal shapeshifter, and an Olympian god of the first generation. Polymorphic Poseidon rules, and is, the saltwater depths who embrace the earth. He came to her once she had discovered and unveiled her own power. Now that Mestra can freely shapeshift into any animal or element, the elemental water god liberates her from her grasping father. Now that she can become a wave of the salt sea, he releases her from her sea of troubles.

Poseidon the Earthshaker swept her away,
exceedingly clever as she was,
and married her on a distant, sea-swept island,
taking her far away from her father over the wine-dark sea.
(Catalogue)

Who is this formidable mate, the one she truly accepted? Poseidon could leap from a steep sea cliff and burst into winged flight like a raptor to soar over the waves. He could stride through vast lands or oceans as an earthshaking white bull, gleaming stallion, or bearded, trident-wielding merman. He could plunge into the watery depths and disappear into his magnificent abode, built in aquamarine caverns,

> Gleaming and sparkling with gold, imperishable forever.
> (*Iliad*)

Land trembled at his footsteps, and when his rage was a swollen flood, he tore mountains apart and shattered ships to splinters.

> Poseidon's heart was angered, and a massive storm rolled in.
> He summoned towering clouds,
> seized his trident and stirred the sea,
> raised up blasts from all the bitter storm winds,
> and covered land and sea with enormous gales.
> Bright day grew dark, and night leapt down from heaven.
> (*Odyssey*)

Yet in an instant, the sea god transforms. He soothes the waters and becomes the hope of sailors, radiating serenity all the way to the horizon.

> Calm beneath clear blue heaven,
> he skims over the tranquil ocean in his chariot,
> giving free rein to pure white horses with golden flowing
>   manes.
> Creatures of the deep rise to frolic around him and rejoice,
> while the sea parts before him in joy.
> (*Vergil, Aeneid; Iliad*)

To intermingle with overlapping images that we have explored for Mestra – shimmering leaves, dappled mind, swirling dance, speaking spring, and waves of entangled roots – now comes the upwelling of ocean depths.

How did Poseidon first perceive Mestra, exceedingly clever as she was? In leaf of oak, ocean wave, bird, filly, mare, doe, serpentine path, or sinuous flood?

Shapeshifting in her quicksilver form of wisdom, betrothed or sold, she too weathered storms within, and she often stood by the shore for solace, listening to the waves, long in thought. Yet in another mood, carefree and secluded, she was lovely in the *thiasos*. Poseidon was attracted by Mestra's circle dances, her long-awaited ceremonies for coming of age, and the springtime radiance that was her gift from the Graces.

> Women alone in nighttime sacrament,
> barefoot, loosened hair,
> unadorned, freshly bathed, worship in the grove.
> Among them, Mestra,
> her face reflected in the welling spring,
> her palm on textured bark,
> her unbound sash billowing on soft breeze,
> bare soles crunching last year's leaves,
> ears entrained to the rushing wind.
> Waves on the sea leap as dashing horses,
> open hands offer first fruits free of stain,
> with teeming grain, bright from the first threshing.
> Wading in the lapping surf, mirrored in the flooding stream,
> down at the water's edge.

In the arms of Poseidon, Artemis withdrew, Aphrodite arrived, and maidenhood gave way to the season of Eros. In a perfect poetic image for Mestra at this moment, love does conquer all.

Eros invincible, you rest unconquered,
sleeping gentle nights on a maiden's soft cheek.
Then up you soar, above vast wilderness and over stormy sea.
(Sophocles, Antigone)

We glimpsed Mesta's girlhood under the auspices of Demeter and witnessed her rejection of any forced transition from *parthenos* to wife. Now Mestra casts off maidenhood, escapes her captors forever, and reveals herself fully fledged. She proceeds through two successful rites of passage, undergoing new transformations into erotic union and childbirth. In doing so, she fulfills a prophecy:

A virgin carried off in secret will give birth to a hero semidivine,
immortal union abundant and ever ageless.
(Corinna)

Aphrodite herself also foreshadowed Mestra's flight with Poseidon over the dusky sea. It happened like this.

One distant long-ago day, Aphrodite yearned for the mortal shepherd Anchises. She flew down to sate her desire – then suddenly needed to explain how she came to be standing in front of him in the wilderness. Looking like the beguiling image of a virgin, sounding like a bewildered maiden, the goddess of love ventured a seductive and convincing tale. She improvised a scene of coming-of-age dance, pretending she had been abducted by a god. Her story is intriguingly like the scrap of myth that describes Mestra's first encounter with Poseidon, when the god "swept her away."

I am not a goddess, but an innocent *parthenos*!
The roving god Hermes swooped down and swept me away,

far from the dance of nymphs and chaste maidens.
We were a chorus performing to an admiring crowd,
when suddenly the passionate god abducted me
and carried me over the wilderness,
and I feared that my feet would never again touch the earth.
So now here I am, lost in the forest, and here we are, all
    alone...
untouched and innocent of love as I am.
(Homeric Hymn to Aphrodite)

In bashful tones, the goddess spins this tale for Anchises' eager ears. Like a marriageable maiden's adventures in an ancient novel, or Helen's unconventional (mis)adventures around Troy, Aphrodite understands being swept away was something to deplore, or relish in the right embrace. Her confused story of immortal rapture is blushingly transparent. By claiming she has caught the roving eye of Hermes, who may have had designs on her chastity but then somehow delivered her to Anchises, Aphrodite is betting that a competitive scenario will spur the shepherd on to action and get him to stop asking questions. Naturally, she is right. From this tryst, though she conceived a child beneath her girdle, Aphrodite did not linger with the shepherd once her longing was fulfilled.

When Mestra is swept away, however, she marries the Sea – in a rare and mystical sense of the word:

Mingling with her desired lover in the deep recesses of
    caverns.
(Homeric Hymn to Aphrodite)

Yet it is also true that Mestra never marries. Not in the sense of a festive wedding, a mortal ideal she would never experience:

In a city broad with seven gates,
the people were delighting in bright festivals and dances.
Companions on a well-wrought chariot
accompanied a bride to her husband,
and the air resounded with their rising wedding songs.

In the distance shone the flames of whirling torches
in the hands of serving maids who led the procession.
Overflowing with delight,
they were followed by revelers, dancers, and musicians,
playing their instruments and singing.

All around rang the men's flowing songs,
to the echo of clear reed pipes.
And in response, the women led out their chorus,
sounding the strumming notes of lyres,
with voices full of desire.
(Hesiod, Shield)

This is how couples wed in the epic lines of lovely legend, with practicality cast aside and romance to the fore. But human marriage, even idealized, is not the model for Mestra's union. As Aphrodite ordains, immortal passion is unbounded by mortal custom. It can be unbounded even by mortal life. Being carried away by a sea god or goddess could mean resurrection as a heroine or hero, via death of previous earthbound existence. In art and myth, it was sometimes imagined that the dead made their final journey over the lashing waves of the sea, with the face of the ocean being their final glimpse of the realm of mortality.

Mestra lives through her otherworldly encounter, to awaken to new life.

There was a rock facing the onrushing ocean, to soften the
incoming waves.
She ran along it and leapt into the sea, yet miraculously
never fell,
but beat the air with newborn wings.
Suddenly she was flying, skimming the surface like a bird.
Her beloved joined her, and together they love to this day,
and on such days the surface of the sea-waves is quiet.
(Metamorphoses)

Entering mystical union, Mestra transcends the limit of death,
for the encounter of Mestra the *daimon* and Poseidon the god
takes the form of *hieros gamos*: sacred marriage and cosmic
sexual coupling. A ritual entering the realms of erotic mysticism
from the dawn of goddess cults in the Fertile Crescent, *hieros
gamos* vitalized the fecundity of the Earth and all life upon
her. Through this rite, Mestra embarks upon a *theoria* toward
newfound esoteric knowledge, continuing her trajectory that
began with shapeshifting. Metamorphosis began once as an
expedient move. Mingling with the cosmic element of water in
sacred marriage, polymorphism now becomes her eternal and
infinite way of being.

*Springtime has come. She raises her winged arms in freedom from the
yoke, and seems to cry out, to the sea, to the sea! Her chariot flanked
with bronze ornaments of trees, lions, and birds draws onward to the
measure of oxen hooves. Worshippers waving branches cry aloud her
wedding song, leading her from her private sanctum. The nuptial bath
is waiting, cold purity of salt sea, with the ritual undressing before
fresh adornment wreathes her for the coming year. Mystically veiled,
a virgin. Unswathed, a wife. Where the dark way opens, moonlight
beckons the procession onward, playing on the tumbled boulders of the
shore. The ocean awaits.*

Hieros gamos transformed celestial Ariadne too, another divine *parthenos* who was a kindred spirit to Mestra. Ariadne joined in sacred union with Dionysus, the shapeshifting god of ecstasy. But first both she and Mestra endured failed wedding rites and found solace on the shore.

Facing the waves, her face turned away,
the *parthenos* is weeping on the shore.
Wading out, wet gown billowing into the waves,
staring out at the horizon, her heart is turbulent with sorrow.
Yet unbeknownst to her,
a god is drawing near.

His *thiasos* approaches to sweep her away,
surrounded with shimmering desire.
With ritual cries they shake their staffs,
with sea snakes they are adorned.
Carrying cult objects, which they now conceal,
preparing to reveal them for her initiation this very night.
Crashing waves, wind on water, and swirling surf
infuse the beach with strange immortal music.
His coming will transform all.
(*Catullus*)

The devotion of a god brings everlasting renown:

She became his immortal consort,
and he embraced her, offering care and protection from
harm.
To give her an everlasting gift, and grant her eternal glory,
he took the diadem she wore on her forehead,
and threw it whirling through the silky heavens,
its jewels transforming to celestial flames.

Look! Her crown still gleams in the night, a heavenly
constellation.
(Metamorphoses)

Mestra and Ariadne, like other heroines we've met, break the
boundary of mortal existence after crisis in a rite of passage.
On the island of Crete, however, Ariadne was originally a
vegetation goddess whose rites focused on seasonal invigoration
and decay. Her thrilling oceanside story of abandonment
and rescue served to entwine her rituals with those of the
grapevine god, Dionysus and reconciled the Olympian deity's
cult with hers. Likewise, Mestra's intrigues and harrowing
escapes were destined to interweave her myth – as a votary
of Demeter, heroine of the sacred grove, celebrated ancestress,
and shapeshifter – with the oceanic cult of Poseidon.

Sexual union was a graphic way to unite more-than-
human beings. When panhellenic gods arrived, local heroines,
daimones, and goddesses erotically encountered them. Many
held their own in what was celebrated as a sensual convergence,
to the enhancement of each other's rites and myths. Coming-
of-age festivals for Ariadne, with displays of nubile grace,
tantalized Dionysus to come to Crete, even as they awakened
desire between Mestra and her divine lover, inviting Poseidon
to Thessaly. Maidens and youths dancing together means the
liminal time for marriage rites draws near:

Come! The dancing ground of Ariadne beckons,
an intricate jewel amid lush and verdant island meadows,
designed of old upon the generous bosom of Earth,
for delicate-robed maidens of lovely tresses,
and chosen youths in vigorous full bloom.
Young men and young women, sought for their charms,
are dancing, gently touching fingers, circling at the wrist.

Can you still see them there?
Their fragrant garments shining, swirling softly.
Every lithesome *parthenos* wears a graceful garland,
Every nimble young man wears a gold blade flashed with
    silver.
Their feet so agile, their hearts rejoicing, darting lightly,
now in spirals, circling and mingling,
now joining and parting like supple waves,
rows crossing rows, intertwining hands.
(Iliad)

Spiral dances pleased the fortunate *parthenos* who moved lithely in her blossoming festival. Supple movements also beckoned gods. Audacious females like Mestra and Ariadne surface valiantly in archaic myth, unfurling tales of passion. As we saw with Aphrodite and her shepherd, erotic unions also transpired when goddesses took initiative and descended to mate with mortal men.

Under the spell of sweet desire, immortal goddesses
sought the beds of mortal men and gave birth to godlike
    children.
(Theogony)

Myths of diverse mating leap across divides and restore gaps in understanding. Ariadne's rapture with Dionysus heals the wounds to her dignity dealt to her by a faithless former love, and blends the image of an abandoned princess into the cult of an epiphanic goddess of Crete. In a similar way, Hades' abduction of Persephone reconciles the apparent contradiction of a deity who was a nymphlike goddess of springtime and a dread goddess of death. Likewise, Mestra's heroine stature is strengthened by her fruitful merging with the god of the sea. For Mestra, *hieros gamos* restores her dignity after her mistreatment from her father, ushers in a consort worthy of her mettle, and secures her a place in mythic memory and ancestral honor.

It is also true that when Mestra the fluid shapeshifter mingled with Poseidon the turbulent Sea, their confluence makes sense of how a roving escape artist ever became a mother, and how a *parthenos* too wily to be caught against her will become a legendary progenitrix. When she had met her match,

> So swiftly, when she desires, a goddess wings her way.
> (*Iliad*)

Generative Eros gives birth to aquatic genealogy when Mestra bears a son, continuing her line of descent from the sole survivors of the primeval Flood.

> Coupling and lingering in Poseidon's arms,
> the embrace of the god is always fruitful.
> When Poseidon swept her away, she bore a son,
> on the far-off, sea-swept island of Cos,
> a child of extraordinary strength, a natural leader of many
>   people.
> His name was Eurypylus, "Wide is the Gate."
> (*Catalogue; Odyssey*)

Her son is named in celebration: she had finally found her way to a union where the gate would never close behind her, but always stand open wide, with a sea-swept *daimon* who found her freedom irresistible.

Archaic song celebrated distinctive mortal-born women like Mestra who mated with gods and gave birth to semidivine offspring. Each of these memorable females was a *parthenos* who mated outside of mortal custom; each was celebrated for her liaison and remembered as heroine in the mythologies of their day. Such glorious females melted the hearts of divine lovers, then founded imposing lineages. As a shapeshifter, Mestra is most curious of them all.

> Desire took the god to mingle in tender love,
> with the maiden of luxuriant tresses,
> lovely in the circle of dancing nymphs.
> Then he appeared to her as a lover,
> on the shore of festive dances.

> From mingling with an immortal,
> she bore a godlike son, child of a *parthenos*.
> She brought to light the cherished infant,
> and he gazed upon the beams of his first dawn.
> (*Iliad*)

In certain rarefied unions, such as the coupling of Mestra with Poseidon or Ariadne with Dionysus, the god does not leave his consort behind. Nor does employ other common mythic diversions, such as a disguise, a cloud of sleep, or abandonment to the machinations of a jealous rival afterward. In fact, the god exalts his beloved and their offspring.

Is this what we call a happy ending? Myth is never so simple.

Considering the proverbial restlessness of gods and goddesses, heroines and *daimones*, it goes without saying that Mestra and Poseidon unite outside of mortal timeframes, customs, or outcomes. The potent promiscuity and amoral predation of gods was legendary and widespread. *Hieros gamos* or not, monogamy was the usual province of no male deity. This included Poseidon and Dionysus, as well as Zeus, Hermes, Apollo, and Hades. Myths of gods shapeshifting to pursue, violate, and impregnate females, including unwilling ones, were legion, and many count as tragedies. Not for the god; for her. Io, Creusa, Medusa, Calisto: the list Arachne wove into her tapestry is long.

Could such a tragedy have been true for Mestra? In the familiar pattern of diminishing this "vixen," one adaptation of Mestra's tale depicted her as a victim of Poseidon and made her shapeshifting power a guilty recompense from the god. We saw this scene in the last chapter; now we can look at it more closely.

> Sold to a master, refusing her fate, and now pursued,
> she cried out to Poseidon who had stolen her virginity,
> beseeching him to save her from enslavement, making
>   recompense.
> Poseidon heard her prayer and changed her form.
> (*Metamorphoses*)

This damsel-in-distress scene rendered Mestra more acceptable to common tastes by foregrounding Poseidon, making Mestra seem pitiful, replacing mutuality or partnership with favor-granting or assault, and erasing her *hieros gamos*. Also completely excised is Mestra's ability to self-transform. That power is given Poseidon instead, implying that if Poseidon helped her once, he was the force behind all her metamorphoses.

But the original manuscripts suggest the opposite: it was only after Mestra had already become a shapeshifter that she vanished with Poseidon, in a transformative meeting of mutual desire.

I believe that when the sea god married her and whisked her away from her sorrows, he extended a sojourn she had already begun, and wisely helped provide refuge far away from her father's halls. To me these words ring true. Like the cryptic pair of "the goddess and the goddess behind," or the shrine with no door or key, all mythic variations both reveal and conceal mysteries – displaying what was told to the many while simultaneously hiding what was known to the few. The unique Mestra who leaps out of archaic myth is not familiar; nor is she acceptable to common tastes. She is no damsel in distress;

she is peculiar, crafty, and brave. Her startling independence, nonconformist risk-taking, non-anthropocentric selves, and unexpected choices are some reasons why I wrote this book. In an era of vanishing wild things, for me she represents, more than anything else, a wild *kore* who rises from the ashes to new life.

Where does she dwell now? There are two ancient ideas, and we may fruitfully contemplate them both.

Is she a *daimon* who watches over human lives?

> A blessed spirit who wanders free,
> journeying over earth and sea,
> veiled in mist, unseen,
> a guardian who protects those who call upon her,
> and keeps them safe from harm.
> (*Works and Days*)

Or is she a heroine, a poignant memory, far distant among the demigods of antiquity?

> Released from troubles, her heart at peace,
> a blithe spirit, she moves among those who live forever,
> far away on the western edge of the earth,
> protected by the tempestuous Ocean,
> at its uttermost limit, on the Isles of the Blest.
> (*Works and Days*)

In the final moments of her story, we look out as she once did, from a promontory over a vast and misty sea, where many figures come and go. Some are outside her; some are within. Each heroine, goddess, and shapeshifter we have met has healed some of the tattered shreds of Mestra's archaic fragments, shedding light through the openings in Mestra's story. In a sense, they are her *thiasos*, who elucidate images of Mestra when she grows obscure and challenging to follow. As noted in the beginning, there are other ways to reconstruct Mestra from the tattered evidence; other ways to assemble her portrait. I represent the heroine who called to me.

The metaphor of being swept away applies to all the senses, evoking mystical flight over a dark sea in mutual captivation. As Dione Naia brought sky god Zeus pure currents of compassionate insight, so Poseidon of sea change brought polymorphic Mestra fathomless inspiration. Together they grew ever more fertile, vivid, and varied. With the strength of her dryad sisters, oracular oaks, Earth spirits, speaking doves, ancestral heroines, priestess guardians, and epiphanic goddesses, Mestra has passed into immortal knowledge. She has been initiated into transcendent mysteries in the fertile ocean of the collective unconscious and immersed in primeval Ocean or Source.

But this could be no final journey, because mythically speaking, Ocean was not just a place. Inside the primordial god Oceanus, beyond the limit of land, beneath the uttermost fount of the unknowable, stirred the origin of all life. To reach this mystical place of origin required a courageous quest coupled with divine power, to find where Oceanus dwelt in *hieros gamos* with leviathan Tethys, his immortal consort of the deep:

Two Titans mingle at the very edge of the generous earth.
Divine Oceanus ever-surging, whence the gods have arisen,
and deathless Tethys, revered mother of immortals,
genesis of raging and rushing rivers, nurse of dread
    goddesses.
In the depths of Oceanus, she coils beneath the horizon.
(*Theogony; Iliad*)

Oceanus, born out of Chaos at the beginning of time, is the vastly older ancestor of Poseidon. His prolific mate Tethys spirals in convoluted dragon form, whence she spawns multitudes of divinities. She lies deep in the dark abyss, coiled beyond human vision or comprehension, giving birth and protecting divinities, especially chthonic goddesses, her fearsome daughters of serpentine spirit.

When Poseidon swept Mestra across the wine-dark sea, he carried her to the realm of Tethys and Oceanus. Shapeshifting Mestra, having taken Poseidon as a lover, embodies multitudes openly and unabashedly now. Ocean and Sea – and Mestra – brim like the collective unconscious, and from their depths rise myths, with their captivating power to carry us to a new place and sweep us away.

What could be more shimmering than a shapeshifter, more *poikile* than the sea? Here at the end, alongside Oceanus and Tethys, Mestra and Poseidon take us deeper into mysteries where there is no single simple truth, for the truth of myth coils deep and thrives in multiplicity.

When Mestra traverses the wine-dark sea, she surpasses limits of human understanding, and crosses the threshold into a new existence beyond place and time. Carried off in secret, swept away, the illusion of linear time ceased, and she experiences seasons and selves in currents, rhythmic tides, sleek cycles of ebb and flow. We leave her in the arms of her beloved Sea, in the lap of a beloved tree goddess, or in a fluid rhythm of their choosing, moving in between at will.

One final image for Mestra unites her two realms of the sacred grove and sounding sea. It is a vision of the *xoanon* transformed, as sentient as the timber of the Argo: the tree goddess soaring as the mast upon a seafaring ship.

Cresting the waves in journeys of her choosing,
the forest goddess treads the waves.
Xoanon as the goddess of the ship, xoanon as the mast.
Grounding the voyaging of sailors

with her memory-roots at home in native soil,
protecting them beneath her robes,
linen sails dancing with the winds.
Her wisdom will guide the ship true,
to arc between wheeling constellations above
and swirling currents below,
passing into the veiled unknown.[18]

On our *theoria* we have flown far. We have searched out the fading traces of Demeter's votary Mestra, elusive heroine of shifting shapes. We have gathered her sacred sisters: honored heroines, liminal nymphs, devious *daimones*, and shining goddesses of many forms.

Let Mestra remain, for those who honor her story, a heroine of transformation. Let versions of her proliferate across mountain ranges, ocean waves, and passages of time:

sheltering us within her protection.

There is a great mystic silence forbidding any ending for Mestra's story, for she is still living it out. Emerging from among the silent women of the past, she rests in winged flight for a moment on a page, or ripples in unseen currents around a story circle.

Throughout Mestra's *theoria* of joy and suffering, she has been an incarnation of animals and elements, and beloved of goddess and god, shimmering in grove and sea. As she found her way through the mysteries of metamorphosis, she embodied many selves. She has been *kore*, votary, princess, pawn, ragged girl, fisherman, *daimon*, bride, and divine lover, on her fluid way to freedom over protean waves of the sea. We have heard of the hero with a thousand faces; she is a heroine who gathers that tradition into her manifold self.

No longer is she voiceless or shackled by fate.

Still, her myth both wounds and heals her. *Parthenos*, survivor, escape artist, trickster, and beast, she still escapes definition. She is a key-bearer, shapeshifting into anything, anything she imagines.

Maiden, mother, mare, heifer, flame, flood, spider, nightingale, sapling. Worshiper and worshiped, she roams now through fathomless depths of the collective unconscious, surfacing only rarely, as a fleeting and precious gift. As an archetype of self-transformation, she has joined the illustrious line of heroines – from which procession she might leap away at any moment as a stag, gush away as a stream, dash off as a young man, dart into the sacred grove, or dive nimbly into the sounding sea.

> Farewell to the dove perched on speaking oak,
> to the serpent spawning her young.
> Farewell to the blossoming dancer,
> to the filly of flashing hooves,
> to the silver-veiled goddess drifting in the swelling surf.

Becoming many, she has come into her own.

Epilogue

Winging upon the springing blossoms of asphodel in the
  meadow,
skimming over the upright tassels of wheat in the field,
running swiftly, racing the winds, never touching the tip of
  bloom or fruit.
(Catalogue)

In dreams last night the ancient ruins beckoned. So in the
morning, bright dawn on the winter solstice, I rose and walked.
Unraveling the trail to a scoured shell of the wind, a half-buried
hall never completed, where the road begins to ebb at forest's
edge, and threads off to the west.

Let the leaf-shadowed cliff of the dryads fall silent,
and fall silent the cool spring that weeps from the rock.
(Odyssey; Greek Anthology)

Were there ever sumptuous feasts here? Tables and bookshelves
grind their knees in the dust, open their palms and spill forth
their contents one by one, distilled into the earthen floor. Every
wall is a window now. Smooth-rubbed floors and timber-
gapped ceilings are a symphony fallen mute; a breath indrawn
just after the last note falls.

A word of tree and a whisper of stone.[19]
(The Ugaritic Epic of Baal)

Into the silence, footsteps. A barefoot girl runs through the
echoing hall. She peers up stairways that stare into vaulted
stone, and dashes out again, weaving through what is fallen
without a glance. Nothing stays her running. Heels flying, she

tumbles into daylight, calling out discovery in clear high tones, to someone invisible on the sundrenched lawn beyond, where bright veils of morning flutter and wing her along.

Begin the song that flies with wings, shining like a swan. The *kore* flashes by. It has been a pleasure to see her, a wistful pleasure dappled with sorrow. To glimpse her darting swiftly toward the sacred grove, milkweed aloft, so lightly that her feet do not disturb the shimmering blossoms, as she disappears.

Journaling Ideas

To engage Mestra, find a safe place for exploration. A favorite notebook or sketchbook is good company. Movement may arise; encourage it. If you choose to do so, revisit what you've written later, in supportive company or glorious solitude, and notice how you've transformed...

- As a votary of a sacred grove (pond, shore, lake, fountain, spring, tree, garden, stone, mountain, meadow), where do you go? If you are seeking such a place, ask a deeper self, one hidden within the one you already know, or ask the landscape around you, listening for an invitation. Let the relationship be revealed as it will. If you already have this place, and have long been devoted to it, consider the newness of inviting Mestra there.
- When you sit quietly in your sacred place and watch wild creatures and elements move, breathe deep and embody the wisdom you see. Feel it in your marrow. What transforms if you invite this practice into your heart? Take time to feel sheltered there, as reality shimmers around you.
- What gifts and vulnerabilities arise when you allow this relationship to be among the most important in your life?
- How do you experience shapeshifting naturally occurring here, around you and inside you, season to season?
- If you traveled to the oracle of Dodona, and consulted the Dove prophetesses in the oak grove, what question would you ask? Ask your sacred place, being open to unexpected replies.
- Mestra introduces us to many allies. Who drew you in? How are you akin to them?
- For you, who is the goddess, and who is the goddess behind?

- What shifts inside if you imagine your life as *theoria*? What portals do you hope to enter more deeply, when Mestra as key-bearer inspires your sacred journey?

- How would it feel to slip the collar or spring open the cage on an outgrown self-image, way of thinking, or habit? Invite the transformative energy of Mestra to help you consider your choices.

- What form does your polymorphic self yearn to become at this moment? Go ahead and journal, sketch, fingerpaint, sculpt, dance, or sing, your choice. Let your answers evolve over time. If you belong to a group, consider sharing these shapes with each other and celebrating the wondrous diversity ranging inside outward appearances.

- Journal some words of gratitude for spiritual community, for moments of *thiasos* you have experienced. This can include many species that will welcome you into their circle, even as they remain wild and rarely glimpsed. Is there a sacred gathering you long to form or find?

- Now that you know many of Mestra's fragments, let's say you've unearthed an ancient papyrus scroll with Mestra's name appearing on it. No one else has ever seen this before. Let your imagination go. What part of her story can you fill in now that you have this clue in your hands? How does it help you understand her journey more deeply?

- Name a self you would like to nourish within your psyche, who might be languishing or fading away. Nonconformist, unbound, powerful in secret, underestimated, crafty, escape artist...what images do you most relate to and wish to fulfill? Invite Mestra to be your guide to invigorate unforeseen possibilities.

- Radical transformation is a natural part of the human life cycle, especially for women. Yet it often holds the unexpected in its hands. In what unforeseen ways are you experiencing metamorphosis now?

- At the end of her known story, Mestra's path is open; open to possibilities, where she goes into the realm of mystery. How and where do you see her? What transformative potential is she living out, and gesturing toward for you?

Notes

1   My translations of original Ancient Greek and Latin sources are creative improvisations upon ancient texts, freely mingled and arranged in collage form. Complete (and more literal) editions are listed in the Bibliography and are easy to access online in the *Perseus Digital Library*.

2   For convenient reference when Greek words appear, please see the Glossary.

3   The ancient Aegean insights in Joan V. O'Brien's *The Transformation of Hera* and Jennifer Larson's *Greek Nymphs* inspire my approach to tree and vegetation goddesses, sanctuaries, and sacred groves throughout this book. My imagistic scenes and poems are responses to archaic artifacts from Greece and Cyprus, many of which are gathered in *The Transformation of Hera* and Caroline Jane Tully's *The Cultic Life of Trees in the Prehistoric Aegean, Levant, Egypt, and Cyprus*. Other images come from the sacred landscape of the Cuyahoga Valley.

4   Though this broad-ranging word narrowed and altered over time, I use it in its original, archaic sense.

5   For brevity's sake, the *Catalogue*, possibly from the seventh or sixth century BCE. I rely on the *Catalogue* editions of Richard Hunter, Kirk Ormond, M. L. West, and Glenn W. Most.

6   *Callimachus: Hymn to Demeter*, Hopkinson, 21–22; *The Hesiodic Catalogue of Women and Archaic Greece*, Ormond, 88.

7   *Greek Nymphs*, 50–52.

8   The Journaling Ideas offer some creative suggestions.

9   In *Women Who Run with the Wolves: Myths and Stories of the Wild Woman Archetype*, Clarissa Pinkola Estés raises such questions for the deeper self.

10 *The Transformation of Hera*, 18–29.

11 Oracles selected from the "Dodona Online Lamellae" on the *Dodona Online Blog*.

12 I abbreviate his somewhat skeptical account.

13 *Oxford Classical Dictionary*, "Dodona."

14 As in Luna Shyr's "A Tale of Two Concertos: Whereas the Reality Trembles, Concerto for Percussion and Orchestra by Johannes Maria Staud."

15 *The Transformation of Hera*, 167–171.

16 *The Transformation of Hera*, 5–62; *Greek Nymphs*, 115–117.

17 *The Transformation of Hera,* 29–31.

18 Inspired by Sarah A. Rich's "She Who Treads on Water"; and Chapter 6, "Trees and Boats," of *The Cultic Life of Trees*.

19 *The Cultic Life of Trees*, 126.

Bibliography

Aeschylus I: The Persians, The Seven Against Thebes, The Suppliant Maidens, Prometheus Bound (3rd ed.), edited by David Grene and Richmond Lattimore. University of Chicago Press, 2013.

Aeschylus II: The Oresteia: Agamemnon, The Libation Bearers, The Eumenides (3rd ed.), edited by David Grene and Richmond Lattimore. University of Chicago Press, 2013.

The Ancient Greek Hero in 24 Hours, by Gregory Nagy. Harvard University Press, 2013.

Apollodorus: The Library of Greek Mythology, translated by Robin Hard. Oxford University Press, 2008.

Apollonius of Rhodes: The Voyage of Argo: The Argonautica, 2nd ed., translated by R.V. Rieu. Penguin, 1971.

Asclepiades of Samos and Leonidas of Tarentum: The Poems, by Jerry Clack. Bolchazy-Carducci, 1999.

Athenaeus: Deipnosophists Volume 7, translated by C. B. Gulick. Harvard University Press, 1941.

"An Avian and Aphrodisian Reading of Homer's *Odyssey*," Paul Friedrich. *American Anthropologist* 99.2: 306–220, 1997.

Callimachus: Hymn to Demeter, edited by N. Hopkinson. Cambridge University Press, 1984.

Callimachus: Hecale, Hymns, Epigrams, edited and translated by Dee L. Clayman. Harvard University Press, 2022.

Catullus: The Poems, edited and translated by Peter Whigham. Penguin, 2006.

Cedar Forests, Cedar Ships: Allure, Lore, and Metaphor in the Mediterranean Near East, Sara A. Rich. Archaeopress Archaeology, 2017.

The Cultic Life of Trees in the Prehistoric Aegean, Levant, Egypt, and Cyprus, Caroline Jane Tully. Peeters, 2018.

"Dodona Online Lamellae: Towards a New Edition of the Lamellae of the Oracle at Dodona," https://dodonaonline. com/lamellae/, edited by Pierre Bonnechere and Jan-Mathieu Carbon. *Dodona Online Blog*, 2016.

"Epiphanies and Signs of Power: Minoan Suggestions and Comparative Evidence," Walter Burkert. *Illinois Classical Studies* 29:1–23, 2004.

Euripides I: Alcestis, Medea, The Children of Heracles, Hippolytus (3rd ed.), edited by David Grene and Richmond Lattimore. University of Chicago Press, 2013.

Euripides III: Heracles, The Trojan Women, Iphigenia Among the Taurians, Ion (3rd ed.), edited by David Grene and Richmond Lattimore. University of Chicago Press, 2013.

Gender and Immortality: Heroines in Ancient Greek Myth *and Cult*, Deborah Lyons. Princeton University Press, 1997.

The Georgics: A Poem of the Land. Virgil, edited and translated by Kimberly Johnson. Penguin, 2011.

The Greek Anthology Book 9: The Declamatory Epigrams, translated by W. R. Paton. Harvard University Press, 1917.

Greek Lyric: Anacreon, Anacreontea, Early Choral Lyric, edited by David Campbell. Harvard University Press, 1988.

Greek Lyric: An Anthology in Translation, translated by Andrew M. Miller. Hackett Publishing Company, 1996.

Greek Lyric: Bacchylides, Corinna, and Others, edited by David Campbell. Harvard University Press, 1992.

Greek Lyric: Stesichorus, Ibycus, Simonides, and Others, edited by David Campbell. Harvard University Press, 1991.

Greek Lyrics (revised ed.), translated by Richmond Lattimore. University of Chicago Press, 1960.

Greek Nymphs: Myth, Cult, Lore, Jennifer Larson. Oxford University Press, 2001.

The Hero with a Thousand Faces (3rd ed.), Joseph Campbell. New World Library, 2008.

Herodotus: The Histories (reissue edition) edited by John M. Marincola, translated by Aubrey de Sélincourt. Penguin, 2003.

Hesiod: The Homeric Hymns and Homerica, translated by H. G. Evelyn-White. Harvard University Press, 1914.

Hesiod: The Shield, Catalogue of Women, Other Fragments, edited and translated by Glenn W. Most. Harvard University Press, 2018.

Hesiod: Theogony, Works and Days, Shield (2nd ed.), translated by Apostolos N. Athanassakis. Johns Hopkins University Press, 2004.

The Hesiodic Catalogue of Women and Archaic Greece, Kirk Ormond. Cambridge University Press, 2014.

The Hesiodic Catalogue of Women: Constructions and Reconstructions, Richard Hunter. Cambridge University Press, 2005.

The Hesiodic Catalogue of Women: Its Nature, Structure, and Origins, M. L. West. Oxford University Press, 1985.

The Homeric Hymns (2nd ed.), translated by Apostolos N. Athanassakis. Johns Hopkins University Press, 2004.

The Homeric Hymn to Demeter: Translation, Commentary, and Interpretive Essays, edited by Helene P. Foley. Princeton University Press, 1994.

Horace: The Complete Odes and Epodes, translated by David West. Oxford University Press, 2008.

The Iliad of Homer, translated by Richmond Lattimore. University of Chicago Press, 2011.

Landscapes, Gender, and Ritual Space: The Ancient Greek Experience, Susan Guettel Cole. University of California Press, 2004.

Marriage to Death: The Conflation of Wedding and Funeral Rituals in Greek Tragedy, Rush Rehm. Princeton University Press, 2019.

The Odyssey of Homer, translated by Richmond Lattimore. Harper Perennial, 2007.

Ovid: Metamorphoses, translated by Rolfe Humphries. Indiana University Press, 2018.

The Oxford Classical Dictionary (3rd ed.), edited by Simon Hornblower and Antony Spawforth. Oxford University Press, 1996.

Pausanias: Description of Greece: Arcadia, Boeotia, Phocis, and Ozolian Locri, translated by W. H. S. Jones. Harvard University Press, 1935.

Perseus Digital Library (online), Gregory Crane and Tufts University. Available at https://www.loc.gov/item/lcwaN0003879/. Tufts University, 2001-.

Plato: The Symposium, edited and translated by Christopher Gill. Penguin, 2013.

Pliny the Elder: Natural History: A Selection (revised ed.), translated by John F. Healy. Penguin, 2004.

The Presocratics, edited by Philip Wheelwright. Prentice Hall, 1997.

"Putting the Women Back into the *Hesiodic Catalogue of Women*," Lillian Daugherty. In Vanda Zajko and Miriam Leonard, eds., *Laughing with Medusa: Classical Myth and Feminist Thought*, 297–325. Oxford University Press, 2006.

Shapeshifting into Higher Consciousness: Heal and Transform Yourself and Our World with Ancient Shamanic and Modern Methods, Llyn Roberts. Moon Books, 2011.

"'She Who Treads on Water': Religious Metaphor in Seafaring Phoenicia," Sara A. Rich. *Ancient West and East* 11:19–34, 2010.

Sophocles I: Oedipus the King, Oedipus at Colonus, Antigone (3rd ed.), edited by David Grene, Richmond Lattimore, Mark Griffith, and Glenn Most. University of Chicago Press, 2013.

Sophocles II: Ajax, The Women of Trachis, Electra, Philoctetes, The Trackers (3rd ed.), edited by David Grene, Richmond Lattimore, Mark Griffith, and Glenn Most. University of Chicago Press, 2013.

A Spell in the Forest, Book 1: Tongues in Trees, Roselle Angwin. Moon Books, 2021.

Staff of Laurel, Staff of Ash: Sacred Landscapes in Ancient Nature Myth, Dianna Rhyan. Moon Books, 2023.

"A Tale of Two Concertos: Whereas the Reality Trembles, Concerto for Percussion and Orchestra by Johannes Maria Staud," Luna Shyr. *The Cleveland Orchestra Spotlight*, Winter 2023: 30–32.

The Transformation of Hera: A Study of Ritual, Hero, and the Goddess in the Iliad, Joan V. O'Brien. Rowman & Littlefield, 1993.

"Trees and Power in Aegean Art," Caroline Tully. *The Ancient Near East Today: Current News About the Ancient Past*, https://www.asor.org/anetoday/2019/06/Trees-and-Power-Aegean-Art/. Friends of the American Society of Overseas Research 7.6, June 2019.

Virgil: The Aeneid, translated by W. F. Jackson Knight. Penguin, 1958.

Women Who Run with the Wolves: Myths and Stories of the Wild Woman Archetype, Clarissa Pinkola Estés. Random House, 1995.

Glossary

Catalogue (*Katalogia*) – A commemorative list. In Mestra's case, an archaic, now-fragmentary genealogical poem associated with Hesiod, describing women of the distant past who were destined to become heroines.

Daimon – A spirit, goddess, nymph, sorceress, or heroine; also a deep-seated emotion, impulse, force of nature, supernatural agent of fate, or divinity who impacted humans on a visceral level.

Dryad – A tree's life energy; a nymph embodied in and uniquely joined with the tree she ensouled. Aligned with naiad (water nymph), and the wild aspect of *parthenos*.

Erysichthon – His name means Earth-Tearer; the alternate form Aithon signifies someone Burning with Hunger.

Heroine – A woman who performed memorable deeds and gained remembrance in myth, poetry, or cult. She may mate with a god and bear semidivine offspring.

Hieros gamos – Sacred marriage or cosmic sexual union; mystical coupling with a deity or between deities.

Kore – A girl; the archetypal Girl in myth, poetry, and art; a cult name for Persephone.

Mestra – Her name means Cunning or Clever; the alternate form Hypermestra suggests she was also unforgettable and exceptionally courted.

Parthenos – Virgin; a social grouping rather than a sexual status for females in archaic Greece, associated with undomesticated vigor, strength, and potential.

Pharmakis – A sorceress skilled in herbs, drugs, and poisons.

Poikilos/e – A shimmering quality; a mood, aura, or mind of shifting, variegated, wavering, complex changeability.

Theoria – A sacred journey undertaken in search of spiritual insight.

Thiasos – A group of worshippers who celebrate sacred rites, gathering to dance, feast, drink, sing, sacrifice, pray, lament, or share in processions.

Xoanon – A venerated trunk of wood, uncarved or roughly carved. A divine image, a focus for awe and devotion, standing in a sacred grove, carried in procession, or enshrined.

Author Biography

Dianna Rhyan is a mythologist and therapist whose work focuses on ancient nature goddesses, tree worship, forgotten voices, and the spirituality of sacred landscapes. As a child she created her first secret language on tablets of clay made from the creek beside her home. In time that language grew into a PhD in Ancient Greek and Latin, and thirty years of college teaching. She has been a visiting scholar on archaeological excavations in Greece and Cyprus, where she explored women's devotion to rural shrines, and studied the ancient evidence for women's veils. When not delving into archaic myth, she can be found on the Cuyahoga Valley trails of Northeast Ohio with her swift-footed husband, her hiking crone companions, and assorted wise dogs.

Acknowledgments

I would like to thank my mentors in classical studies, mythology, and archaeology, especially Jane, Ron, Vivian, June, Stephen, Sarah, Joe, Eliot, Michael, Tim, and Don, for their ceaseless inspiration and challenge. When the tables turned, I surely taught the most gifted, keen, curious, and engaged students any professor has ever known. They come to mind always, on the frontiers of myth and ancient languages, in enthusiastic explorations that made me excited to open the door of every classroom. Boundless appreciation for true friends of rare spirit and dauntless hikers Gloria, Dawna, and Ahna, the warm embrace of Tamar and Lisa, and the enthusiasm of Emily and Chris. Jeff for the referral of a lifetime, and Beth for *not* listening to me at a crucial moment. John and Shelley of WMP, Trails Forever of CVNP, The ADK Mountain Club, and all those who have hiked with me and shared retreats. I am deeply grateful for the entire expert team at Moon Books, especially my insightful and responsive editor Trevor Greenfield, who believed in this project and brought this book to life; and Frank Smecker, whose expertise saw it into polished print. Heartfelt appreciation to readers of drafts, including the perceptive Rachel Patterson, and first readers Mark and Nicholas, who heard the project come into being. Thankfulness and treats for Coco, whose spirit warmed, distracted, and brightened writing days. Immortal awe for sun swept, sea swept, bittersweet Korinthos, washed by harbors, wreathed in sanctuaries, shaded by lemon, pomegranate, pine, laurel, olive, and oak. Heartfelt admiration for the courage and strength of Christine. Profound gratitude for the unfolding gift of adventuring through life with Mark of *phaidimos* mind and questing spirit, *philotimos andras* of largest heart. And finally, ever and always, wonderment for the epic journey (including that remarkable year of Ancient Greek) with *palikari* Nicholas, *thesavraki, pharaki, kai kardia mou.*

You may also like

Dianna Rhyan

STAFF of
LAUREL
STAFF of
ASH

SACRED LANDSCAPES IN
ANCIENT NATURE MYTH

At the crossroads of nature and human imagination, ancient goddesses, outcasts, poets, and heroes reveal living myths in sacred landscapes.

978-1-80341-196-5 (paperback)
978-1-80341-197-2 (e-book)

MOON BOOKS
PAGANISM & SHAMANISM

What is Paganism? A religion, a spirituality, an alternative belief system, nature worship? You can find support for all these definitions (and many more) in dictionaries, encyclopaedias, and text books of religion, but subscribe to any one and the truth will evade you. Above all Paganism is a creative pursuit, an encounter with reality, an exploration of meaning and an expression of the soul. Druids, Heathens, Wiccans and others, all contribute their insights and literary riches to the Pagan tradition. Moon Books invites you to begin or to deepen your own encounter, right here, right now.

If you have enjoyed this book, why not tell other readers by posting a review on your preferred book site.

Readers of ebooks can buy or view any of these bestsellers by clicking on the live link in the title. Most titles are published in paperback and as an ebook. Paperbacks are available in traditional bookshops. Both print and ebook formats are available online.

Find more titles and sign up to our readers' newsletter www.collectiveinkbooks.com/paganism

For video content, author interviews and more, please subscribe to our YouTube channel.

MoonBooksPublishing

Follow us on social media for book news, promotions and more:

Facebook: Moon Books

Instagram: @MoonBooksCI

X: @MoonBooksCI

TikTok: @MoonBooksCI